2 in 1

Shadow
Work Journal

+ 13 Shadow Integration Exercises

A Comprehensive Guide to Shadow Work
Transformation and Self-Discovery

Amanda Kimmons

2024

Contents

Introduction

In the labyrinth of the human psyche lies an uncharted terrain — the realm of the shadow. This concealed aspect of our consciousness houses our hidden desires, suppressed emotions, unresolved traumas, and unacknowledged fears. It is the repository of the parts of ourselves we prefer to keep in the dark, aspects we often deny or project onto others. These shadow elements, unexamined and unexplored, can significantly impact our lives, influencing our decisions, relationships, and self-perception.

Welcome to a transformative journey of self-discovery, self-acceptance, and self-empowerment. This book is your guide to shadow work, a profound process of confronting the hidden facets of your being. Over the next 30 days, you will delve deep into the recesses of your psyche, shining a light on the aspects of yourself that have long dwelled in the shadows.

Each day of this journey will be a stepping stone towards self-awareness and self-compassion. You will explore the inner child, uncover core beliefs, heal past traumas, confront fears and insecurities, and identify recurring patterns in your life. You will develop tools to embrace and integrate your shadow aspects, ultimately leading to a more authentic, whole, and empowered self.

But this is not just a solitary endeavor. We invite you to become an active participant, an explorer of your inner world. You will engage in reflective journaling, meditative practices, artistic expression, and transformative exercises. The insights and revelations you encounter on this path will become a mirror reflecting the richness of your inner landscape.

It's essential to remember that shadow work is a continuous, lifelong process. As you take the first step on this journey, you initiate an ongoing exploration of self. The shadows are not to be feared; they are your allies in understanding the full spectrum of your humanity.

As you embark on these 30 days of shadow work, embrace every emotion, face every fear, and welcome every hidden aspect with an open heart. You are about to embark on a profound journey — one that will lead you to a deeper sense of self, personal growth, and a life more aligned with your true nature.

This is your adventure, your odyssey into self. Let the journey begin.

Declaration of intent

I, _____ , at this moment, make a solemn commitment to embark on the transformative journey of shadow work. I recognize the profound importance of this inner exploration, both for my personal growth and the betterment of my life.

I commit to dedicating time and effort to understanding and integrating my shadow aspects. I promise to approach this journey with self-compassion, non-judgment, and openness. I understand that shadow work is a process, and I will not rush or judge myself for the time it takes to explore and heal. I pledge to engage with the provided exercises, journaling prompts, and practices throughout the 28 days.

I commit to maintaining the confidentiality of my own shadow work journey. This process is deeply personal, and I will respect my own boundaries and privacy. I promise to be patient and gentle with myself as I confront difficult emotions and hidden aspects. I will strive to be consistent, but if I falter, I will practice self-forgiveness and continue.

Signature: _____

Start Date: _____

Completion Date: _____

Chapter 1
The Concept of Shadows

In the realm of self-discovery and personal development, few subjects are as profound and transformative as delving into the shadows of one's psyche. The concept of shadows, often attributed to the renowned Swiss psychiatrist Carl Jung, is a foundational element in understanding the human psyche's complexities and the path to self-awareness.

Understanding the Shadow Self

The "shadow self" encompasses hidden, repressed aspects of one's personality. These include various emotions, traits, desires, and fears that people consciously or unconsciously conceal from themselves and others.

Recognizing the shadow self is the first step in the journey of self-discovery, signifying that personalities are multifaceted. Understanding the shadow self requires introspection, self-reflection, and a willingness to confront uncomfortable truths. By making the darkness conscious, as Jung described it, we unlock the potential for personal growth, self-acceptance, and emotional healing.

Why Shadow Work Matters

Shadow work is essential as hidden elements continue to influence thoughts, feelings, and behaviors unconsciously. Unacknowledged shadows can lead to self-sabotaging patterns, conflicts in relationships, and health issues. Engaging in shadow work brings these concealed elements into the light of consciousness, granting the power to understand and transform them.

A Path to Self-Awareness

Shadow work is a path to profound self-awareness. It involves introspection and self-reflection, leading to a better understanding of motivations, reactions, behaviors, and insights into the root causes of challenges and conflicts.

Understanding the shadow self provides a gateway to heightened self-awareness, which is essential for personal growth. It allows individuals to confront limitations, dismantle self-imposed barriers, and release the grip of past traumas, leading to a greater sense of well-being.

The Impact on Emotional Well-being

Engaging in shadow work profoundly impacts emotional well-being. It empowers individuals to heal and integrate unresolved emotions and traumas, leading to emotional resilience. It also equips them to handle stress, anxiety, and emotional distress with understanding and self-compassion.

Shadow work alleviates emotional burdens stemming from suppressed emotions and unresolved traumas, fostering inner peace and emotional freedom. As individuals work through their shadows, they release emotional baggage, resulting in a greater sense of well-being.

Enhanced Relationships

Shadow work significantly impacts relationships, as our shadows often project onto others, leading to misunderstandings and conflicts. Through shadow work, individuals become more aware of these projections, resulting in healthier, more authentic, and vulnerable connections.

In summary, shadow work enables individuals to confront concealed personality aspects, fostering self-awareness, emotional well-being, and improved relationships. It empowers individuals to transcend self-imposed limitations, release emotional burdens, and cultivate inner peace. The significance of shadow work becomes increasingly evident on the journey of self-discovery, offering a transformative path to holistic well-being and personal growth.

The Path to Self-Discovery

In personal transformation and psychological well-being, self-reflection and self-awareness are crucial foundations for shadow work. They enable us to explore our shadow self intentionally, providing insights into our concealed psyche. This journey of self-discovery is guided by self-reflection as the map and self-awareness as the compass, leading to a deeper understanding of our true selves.

The Essence of Self-Reflection

Self-reflection is a mirror that allows us to scrutinize our thoughts, feelings, and actions. It involves peering into the pool of our consciousness to examine the ripples generated by our choices and experiences. This process provides clarity about the motivations and intentions driving our lives. It is not just about reviewing the past but also examining the present moment to gain insights into the future. Self-reflection empowers us to question our beliefs, values, and desires, unveiling layers of our identity and exposing concealed truths.

It is not merely about looking back but examining the present moment and gleaning insights for the future. It empowers us to question our beliefs, values, and desires, unveiling the layers of our identity and exposing the truths that may have long remained concealed.

The Power of Self-Awareness

Self-awareness serves as the lighthouse, illuminating our inner landscape and revealing hidden aspects of our personality. It enables us to observe our thoughts, emotions, and behaviors as they occur, deepening our self-understanding. This awareness extends beyond the surface of our consciousness, delving into the depths of our subconscious mind. It allows us to navigate the intricate web of our emotions, recognizing the undercurrents of our feelings and the motivations driving our actions. Self-awareness empowers us to make conscious choices, fostering authenticity and alignment with our true selves.

The Ripple Effect

As we become more attuned to ourselves, we become more empathetic toward others. This heightened empathy and understanding create a ripple effect that extends to our relationships, communities, and the broader world.

In our interactions with others, self-awareness enables us to handle conflicts gracefully and compassionately. We recognize the interconnectedness of all living beings and work towards fostering understanding and harmony. Our authentic presence inspires those around us.

The Role of the Therapist

Shadow work is challenging for individuals with deep psychological trauma. In this context, the therapist plays a crucial role in supporting clients during shadow work.

1. **Creating a Safe and Secure Environment:** The therapist ensures clients can explore their shadows without re-traumatization. This involves setting clear boundaries, ensuring confidentiality, and providing unwavering support.

2. **Trauma-Informed Approach:** The therapist's choices in therapy are informed by understanding potential triggers and sensitivities related to the client's trauma history, maintaining the client's emotional safety throughout the shadow work process.

3. **Building Trust and Rapport:** The therapist builds a solid therapeutic alliance by demonstrating empathy, consistency, and reliability.

4. **Ego Strength and Stabilization:** Therapists help clients develop ego strength and emotional stabilization, especially when dealing with deep trauma. This support is crucial as clients may experience intense emotional upheaval during the shadow work process. The therapist provides coping strategies to manage these emotions effectively.

5. **Gradual Exposure:** Shadow work may involve exploring painful and repressed memories. Therapists guide clients through this process with sensitivity, often using incremental exposure techniques to avoid overwhelming the client. This approach helps the client process trauma without being retraumatized.

6. **Integration and Healing:** The therapist's ultimate goal is to facilitate the integration of shadow aspects into the client's whole self. This process promotes healing, self-acceptance, and personal growth. It often involves addressing core wounds related to trauma and working through them in a supportive and structured manner.

7. **Monitoring and Adjusting:** Therapists continuously monitor the client's progress and emotional well-being, prepared to adjust the pace and depth of shadow work to ensure the client's safety and progress.

8. **Referring to Specialists:** In some cases, clients with deep psychological trauma may require specialized trauma therapy in conjunction with shadow work. Therapists must recognize when such referrals are necessary for the client's well-being.

In summary, the therapist's role in shadow work with clients who have deep psychological trauma is multifaceted, emphasizing creating a safe environment, trauma-informed care, trust-building, ego strength development, gradual exposure, integration, ongoing monitoring, and referrals when necessary. Therapists play a pivotal role in supporting clients with trauma on their journey toward healing, self-discovery, and the integration of their shadows

Chapter 2
Unveiling the Shadows

Shadows, often elusive and concealed, are essential components of our psyche. To engage with them effectively, we must first unveil their presence.

Identifying Your Shadows

Before delving into the nuances of shadow work, it's crucial to recognize and identify these elusive facets of our being.

The first step in identifying your shadows is acknowledging their existence. This may seem deceptively simple, but it requires a degree of introspection and self-awareness that many people find challenging. It demands a willingness to confront uncomfortable truths about oneself and to examine concealed aspects.

To identify your shadows, consider the following questions:

Facing Your Fears

1. What do you fear?

2. What are you afraid of, and why? What triggers intense emotional reactions in you?

3. What are recurring themes or patterns in your life?

4. What aspects of your personality do you hide from others or deny to yourself?

The result is a newfound sense of empowerment and courage. By acknowledging and confronting these fears, you create an opportunity for personal growth and transformation. You can work on gradually desensitizing yourself to these fears, develop strategies to cope with them, or even overcome them entirely. This process enables you to navigate life with greater confidence resilience, and a reduced impact of these fears on your daily decisions and actions, ultimately leading to a more fulfilling and authentic life.

Common Shadow Traits

While unique to each individual, some shadow traits are commonly associated with the shadow self. These traits can serve as valuable indicators when identifying your shadows:

- **Repressed Emotions:** Shadows often encompass emotions individuals have suppressed or denied, such as repressed anger, sadness, or fear.
- **Unresolved Trauma:** Past traumatic experiences can cast long shadows over our lives, leading to shadow traits like hypervigilance, avoidance, or emotional numbing.
- **Projection:** Shadows frequently project onto others, causing misunderstandings and conflicts when we unconsciously attribute our hidden traits or emotions to them.
- **Self-Sabotage:** Behaviors that undermine goals and well-being often find their roots in the shadows, including procrastination, self-criticism, or self-destructive habits.
- **Unwanted Patterns:** Recurring relationship patterns can indicate shadow involvement, such as consistently choosing the same type of partner or experiencing the same conflicts.

Recognizing Projection

Projection, a defense mechanism, is when individuals attribute their own unconscious thoughts, feelings, and qualities to others, allowing them to cope with uncomfortable or unwanted aspects of their psyche by attributing them to someone else. It can take various forms:

- Positive Projection occurs when people project their positive qualities onto others, disowning their potential for those traits.
- Negative Projection occurs when, more commonly, individuals project their fears, insecurities, and negative traits onto others, attributing these qualities to those around them.
- Projection is a central element in shadow work because it directs attention to concealed aspects of one's personality. Recognizing projection involves self-reflection, identifying the source, embracing self-acceptance, and shadow integration to reclaim disowned traits and emotions. This process fosters a more authentic and balanced self.

Projection in Relationships

In relationships, projecting our shadows onto others significantly impacts interactions and can lead to misunderstandings, conflicts, and emotional turmoil. For example, accusing a partner of untrustworthiness might arise from unresolved trust issues or past betrayals within the accuser.

Recognizing projection is a valuable skill in shadow work. Here are practical steps to help identify and work with projection:

- **Mindful Self-Reflection:** Pause to reflect on your emotions, judgments, and reactions, considering if you might be projecting your traits onto others.
- **Journaling:** Keep a projection journal to document instances, including the emotions or traits projected and the circumstances. This journal aids self-awareness.
- **Therapeutic Guidance:** Seek a trained therapist's assistance if you find it challenging to deal with projection. Therapists offer valuable insights and techniques.
- **Communication:** Foster open, honest communication with those close to you to understand better how projection affects your relationships.

Shadow Archetypes

Within the vast human psyche lies a realm of captivating exploration known as shadow archetypes. Let us talk about these hidden personas, revealing their significance, manifestations, and transformative potential when integrated into conscious awareness.

Understanding Shadow Archetypes

Shadow archetypes represent concealed facets of our personality that contrast with our conscious identity. These encompass positive and negative traits, emotions, and patterns in the shadows due to societal conditioning or personal denial. Introduced by Carl Jung in psychology, the concept of the shadow reveals these hidden elements, spanning individual and collective aspects.

Shadow archetypes act as guardians of uncharted psychic territory. They house traits and qualities deemed undesirable, repressed, or disowned, yet offer untapped potential for personal growth and self-discovery. These archetypes are dormant or underdeveloped aspects of our personality, holding unexpressed creativity, strength, and wisdom.

Common Shadow Archetypes

The Victim: Characterized by a sense of powerlessness and a tendency to blame external circumstances for suffering, this archetype may manifest as self-pity and avoidance of responsibility.

The Perfectionist: Marked by an obsessive need for flawlessness, leading to self-criticism and an inability to accept imperfection, often resulting in stress and anxiety.

The Saboteur: Represents an inner critic undermining one's goals and potential due to self-doubt, leading to self-sabotage in personal and professional growth.

The Procrastinator: Embodies a tendency to delay tasks due to fear of failure or perfectionism, potentially hindering personal and professional progress.

The Inner Critic: A relentless, self-critical voice that judges and condemns actions, fueling feelings of inadequacy and self-doubt.

The People-Pleaser: Marked by an excessive need for approval and avoidance of conflict, often resulting in burnout and difficulty establishing boundaries.

The Control Freak: Compulsively needs to control situations or people due to a fear of uncertainty, leading to trust issues and difficulties with adaptability.

The Abandonment Wound: Linked to the fear of rejection and abandonment, stemming from past experiences, potentially leading to clingy behavior and difficulties in establishing healthy relationships.

The Inner Child: Represents childlike aspects of the self, including innocence and vulnerability, and can lead to emotional wounds when disowned.

The Prostitute: Involves compromising values or principles for external gain, causing inner conflict and a diminished sense of self-worth.

The Rescuer: Compulsively helps and saves others, often at the expense of personal well-being, potentially leading to codependency and emotional drain.

The Addict: Involves compulsive attachments to substances, behaviors, or relationships, leading to self-destructive consequences and a cycle of dependence.

The Tyrant: Represents the ruthless and controlling aspects of the self, often creating a hostile or toxic environment in relationships and interpersonal dynamics.

Recognizing Shadow Archetypes

Recognizing Shadow Archetypes is a crucial but sometimes challenging initial step in shadow work. It requires a multi-faceted approach that includes *self-reflection, introspective questions, feedback from trusted individuals, dream analysis,* and *therapeutic guidance.* Through self-reflection, one can identify recurring patterns, emotions, and unexplained behaviors that point to the presence of shadow archetypes. Asking introspective questions, such as understanding qualities or behaviors disapproved of in others or recognizing patterns leading to undesirable outcomes, can shed light on concealed aspects of the psyche.

Feedback from close friends and family can provide valuable insights into one's shadow archetypes, as external perspectives can often reveal what is hidden within. Paying attention to recurring themes in dreams, as they frequently reflect unconscious shadow aspects, is another means of identifying these archetypes. Finally, seeking therapeutic guidance from a trained therapist or counselor can offer a safe environment for self-exploration and provide professional assistance in recognizing, understanding, and working with shadow archetypes.

Self-Reflection Questionnaire

What recurring patterns in my life do I find frustrating or confusing?

_____

_____

_____

Are there any emotions I frequently experience but can't easily explain or attribute to specific circumstances?

_____

_____

_____

_____

Do I notice any behaviors or reactions that seem out of character for me or contrary to my conscious intentions?

_____

_____

_____

_____

What situations or interactions trigger intense emotional responses that I find hard to control or understand?

_____

_____

_____

_____

Are there aspects of my personality that I keep hidden from others and even from myself?

_____

_____

_____

_____

Do I tend to judge or criticize certain traits or behaviors in others?

_____

_____

_____

_____

What aspects of my life consistently lead to outcomes I do not desire or expect?

_____

_____

_____

Introspective Mind Map

Instructions: Create a mind map to visually explore your reactions to qualities or behaviors in others and patterns in your life that lead to undesirable outcomes.

Feedback Grid

Instructions: Create a grid to document feedback received from trusted friends and family members.

Person's Name	Qualities/Behaviors Noticed	Situations/Patterns Observed	Impact on Relationship

Dream Analysis

Instructions: Use this blank page to record (write or draw) and analyze recurring themes in your dreams related to shadow aspects. Describe your dreams and the patterns you notice.

Chapter 3
The Mirror of Relationships

In the intricate dance of human connections, relationships serve as mirrors reflecting the depths of our psyche. We will explore how relationships reveal concealed aspects of our shadow self and their transformative power.

Shadows in Relationships

Relationships offer unique opportunities for self-discovery and personal growth. They reflect our traits, emotions, and patterns, often bringing hidden aspects to light.

Family Dynamics: Where It All Begins

Family, often seen as life's cornerstone, is where we take our first steps, learn foundational values, and form early attachments. However, family dynamics can cultivate shadow aspects. Let's explore how family dynamics play a crucial role in shadow development:

1. **Parental Shadows:** Parents serve as our first mirrors and behavioral models. If parents have unresolved wounds or concealed aspects, we may inherit or internalize these shadows.
   Example: A parent's self-esteem issues may pass on patterns of self-doubt or insecurity.

2. **Siblings and Rivalries:** Sibling dynamics are a significant arena for shadow projection and rivalry. Siblings compete for parental attention, revealing competitive shadow archetypes (Victim, Saboteur, Rescuer). Unconscious mirroring of each other's shadows can persist into adulthood.

3. **Generational Patterns:** Family dynamics extend to generational patterns, including behaviors and belief systems. Unresolved shadows, like substance abuse or unhealthy relationships, perpetuate across generations. Recognizing and addressing these patterns is crucial for fostering healthier family dynamics.

4. **Attachment Styles:** Attachment styles, pivotal in adult relationships, originate in family dynamics. Secure attachments result from consistent care, while insecure attachments stem from inconsistent care or neglect. Insecure attachments manifest in adult relationships, leading to shadows like jealousy, fear of abandonment, or controlling behavior.

Friendships: Mirrors of Self-Perception

Friendships, as voluntary connections, offer opportunities for personal growth and self-awareness. They act as mirrors reflecting our self-perception, both strengths and shadows.

1. **Projection and Reflection:** Struggling with inadequacy may lead to projecting self-doubt onto a friend. Friendships reflect our traits, revealing aspects not readily recognized.

2. **Shared Shadows:** Close friendships often form with individuals sharing similar insecurities. Shared shadows can deepen connection but may lead to co-dependency or enabling behavior.

3. **Growth and Support:** Authentic friendships support self-awareness and personal growth. Open conversations with friends help identify projections and shadow aspects. Friends offer different perspectives, challenge assumptions, and encourage facing concealed qualities.

4. **Toxic Friendships:** Unaddressed shadows in friendships can lead to toxicity. Toxic friendships manifest as manipulation, jealousy, or lack of authenticity. Projection and shared shadows become sources of conflict rather than growth opportunities.

Love and Relationships as a Mirror

Love is a complex aspect of human life, influencing us in beautiful and challenging ways. Let's explore how love and relationships are potent mirrors, reflecting our inner world, shadow aspects, and growth potential.

The Mirror of Attraction

1. **Projection and Idealization:** Attraction often begins with projecting an idealized self-image onto our partner. This projection can reveal desires, hopes, and unacknowledged shadows.
   Example: Longing for adventure but suppressing it may lead to attraction to someone embodying adventurous qualities.

2. **Shadow Projections:** Idealized projections may expose our own concealed fears or insecurities.
   Example: Projecting bravery onto a partner may reflect our own hidden fears.

Conflict as a Mirror

1. **Conflict as a Teacher:** Relationship conflict serves as a teacher, illuminating unacknowledged fears and insecurities. Emotional intensity during conflicts highlights suppressed emotions.

2. **Revealing Unresolved Shadows:** Conflicts may expose shadows, like a fear of abandonment rooted in past experiences.

3. **Opportunities for Resolution:** Addressing shadows in conflicts offers opportunities for personal growth and relationship enhancement. Conflict resolution deepens understanding and fosters harmonious dynamics.

Attachment Styles and the Mirror of Love

1. **Secure Attachment:** Those with a secure attachment style navigate love with a positive self-view, comfortable with intimacy and independence.

2. **Insecure Attachment Styles:** Insecure attachment styles may manifest in behaviors linked to shadows, like fear of abandonment in anxious attachment. Insecurities and past experiences influence attachment styles.

Intimacy and Vulnerability

1. **Revealing Shadows:** True intimacy requires vulnerability, unveiling fears, insecurities, and suppressed emotions. Sharing shadows creates profound intimacy.

2. **The Fear of Rejection:** Fear of rejection for concealed aspects can be a hurdle rooted in past experiences or societal expectations.

Healing and Growth Through Love

1. **Embracing Authenticity:** Authentic love encourages embracing our true selves, shadows included. Foster's self-acceptance and mutual understanding.

2. **Shared Growth:** Love becomes fertile ground for mutual growth, especially when couples engage in shadow work together. Supporting each other's journeys fosters self-discovery.

3. **Transcending Shadows:** Love's mirror helps transcend shadows by acknowledging and integrating concealed aspects. More authentic and fulfilling relationships can be cultivated through self-awareness and growth.

Love and relationships are profound mirrors, reflecting our inner world, shadow aspects, and potential for growth and transformation.

Healing through Relationships

Engaging in shadow work within relationships can lead to profound healing. To facilitate this healing:

Practice Self-Reflection

- When projecting onto others, ask, *"What does this say about me?"*
- Take ownership of shadows to initiate the healing process.

Communication and Vulnerability

- Foster healing through open and honest communication.
- Approach conversations with empathy and active listening.
- Embrace vulnerability for deeper connections and potential healing.

Forgiveness and Compassion

- Use forgiveness to free yourself from resentment and anger.
- Cultivate compassion by extending understanding and kindness.

Boundaries and Self-Care

- Establish healthy boundaries for well-being and growth.
- Prioritize self-care to nurture physical, emotional, and spiritual needs.

Transformational Process

- Healing through relationships requires courage, self-reflection, and vulnerability.
- True healing begins with embracing the power of relationships for transformative change.

Chapter 4

The Shadow Work Process

Awareness is indeed the initial and essential stage in the process of shadow work, a topic we've explored in more detail in previous chapters. But what happens once we've successfully uncovered our hidden shadow selves? This is where the journey of shadow work takes its next significant step.

The Four Stages of Shadow Work

Awareness

Awareness is the initial and essential stage in the process of shadow work. Recognize hidden aspects like emotions, fears, and patterns. Confront denial and societal conditioning through self-reflection.

Acceptance: Embracing Your Shadow

Acceptance is the second stage of shadow work. Embrace shadows with compassion and non-judgment — practice self-compassion, mindfulness, journaling, therapy, creative expression, dialogue, and visualization.

Acceptance sets the stage for transformation and integration, paving the way for a deeper understanding of concealed aspects.

Integration. Tools and Techniques: Merging the Shadow with the Self

Integration is the transformative stage where you actively merge your shadow aspects with your conscious self. Here's a practical exercise for shadow integration.

Mirror Work

Mirror Work, popularized by Louise Hay, is a powerful self-reflective exercise that encourages you to stand in front of a mirror, gaze into your own eyes, and engage in a compassionate dialogue with yourself.

How to Do It:

1. **Eye Contact:** Stand before the mirror, make eye contact, and acknowledge the connection with your inner self.
2. **Dialogue:** Engage in self-compassionate dialogue, affirming acceptance, embrace, and integration.
3. **Affirmation:** Address your shadow aspects, visualizing them embraced in warm, accepting light.
4. **Emotional Awareness:** Pay attention to emotions, allowing them to flow naturally.

Examples of Mirror Work:

Embracing Vulnerability: *"I accept and integrate my vulnerability. It is a source of strength and authenticity in me."*

Transforming Fear: *"I accept and integrate my fear. It has guided me and protected me in the past. Now, I choose to transform it into courage."*

Balancing Anger: *"I accept and integrate my anger. It is my passionate drive for change and growth. I now harness it positively."*

Inner Dialogue

Inner Dialogue is a practice involving conversations with your shadow aspects.

How to Do It:

1. **Medium:** Decide if you prefer journaling or speaking aloud. Choose the method most comfortable for you.

2. **Select Shadow Aspect:** Choose a specific shadow aspect like your inner critic, vulnerability, or anger for exploration.

3. **Initiate Conversation:** Start the dialogue by addressing your chosen shadow aspect. Pose open-ended questions and express curiosity about its role in your life.

4. **Active Listening:** Actively listen to the responses that arise. Allow your shadow aspect to express itself without judgment.

Examples of Inner Dialogue:

- **Inner Critic:** *"Why do you criticize me so harshly?"* Explore its intentions and motivations, like the desire to protect you from perceived mistakes.

- **Vulnerability:** *"What are your fears, and how do you serve me?"* Engage in a conversation that uncovers vulnerability's concerns and its role in fostering authenticity.

- **Anger:** *"What drives you, and how can we work together constructively?"* Discover how anger can be a force for positive change and empowerment.

Collage Creation

Collage creation is a personal method for visually representing the integration of shadow aspects.

How to Do It:

1. **Select Elements:** Choose images, words, and symbols representing known and concealed qualities.

2. **Arrange Visually:** Create a visual arrangement to symbolize harmony between conscious and shadow self.

Examples:

- **Strength and Vulnerability:** Blend an oak tree for strength with a butterfly for vulnerability.

- **Resilience:** Feature a phoenix rising from ashes to depict bouncing back from adversity.

- **Balance of Light and Dark:** Use the yin and yang symbol to balance light and dark aspects.

- **Personal Experiences:** Add images related to significant challenges you've faced.

Soul Collage

Soul Collage is an introspective method for shadow work.

Creating Your Deck:

1. **Gather Materials:** Collect magazines, images, words, and symbols resonating with you.
2. **Select Your Committee:** Create cards representing different aspects, including your shadow self.
3. **Card Creation:** Choose images like a fiery dragon to represent anger. Combine with others for a holistic portrayal.

Using Your Deck:

- **Meditation:** Select a card for meditation, letting the image guide insights into concealed qualities.
- **Self-Reflection:** Consult your deck when facing challenges. Choose a card mirroring your state for self-reflection.

Examples of Soul Collage:

- **The Shadow Card:** If rooted in fear, create a card with a dark forest or a person with a hidden face symbolizing concealed fears.

Shadow Play

Shadow Play is a visualization exercise for integrating conscious and shadow aspects.

Performing Shadow Play:

4. **Relaxation:** Use deep breathing to calm your mind and body.
5. **Visualization:** Close your eyes and visualize your conscious self as light and your shadow as darkness.
6. **Merging Imagery:** Visualize these figures coming closer, merging into a unified entity.
7. **Feel the Unity:** Focus on emotional and psychological sensations, feeling the integration.

Examples of Shadow Play:

- **Confronting Fear:** Merge your conscious self and fear-laden shadow into a figure embodying courage.
- **Embracing Vulnerability:** Blend your conscious self and guarded shadow into a figure radiating openness, embracing vulnerability.
- **Accepting Imperfection:** Merge your conscious self and perfectionist shadow into a figure balancing excellence with humanity.

Role Reversal

Role Reversal is a written exercise to explore the world from the perspective of a specific shadow aspect.

Engaging in Role Reversal:

Choose a Shadow Aspect: Select a shadow aspect like inner critic, vulnerability, anger, etc.

Written Exploration: Find a quiet space, open your journal, and write from the perspective of the chosen shadow aspect.

Embrace Empathy: Fully immerse yourself in its worldview without judgment.

Feelings and Motivations: Explore your chosen shadow aspect's feelings, fears, desires, and motivations.

Examples of Role Reversal:

Inner Critic: Describe its role as a protective force, pointing out flaws for your well-being.

Vulnerability: Explain its perception of a world filled with potential threats and its courage in allowing authenticity.

Anger: Describe the world through the lens of frustration and the desire for positive change.

Creative Expression

Creative Expression is a therapeutic approach using art to externalize and explore your shadow aspects.

Practicing Creative Expression:

1. **Select a Medium:** Choose a creative medium like painting, writing, or music that resonates with you.
2. **Set the Intention:** Before starting, set the intention to express your shadow aspects and explore concealed qualities.
3. **Allow Flow:** Let thoughts and emotions flow freely during the creative process without overthinking or judgment.
4. **Visual Symbols:** Use visual symbols to represent your shadow aspect in art. For vulnerability, paint a figure with an open heart.
5. **Writing Narratives:** Create characters or narratives embodying your shadow qualities to explore their inner worlds, fears, and desires.
6. **Musical Emotions:** Compose music reflecting the emotions and experiences associated with your shadow, symbolizing the integration process.

Examples of Creative Expression:

- **Vulnerability in Art:** Paint a symbol of openness, like a figure shedding protective layers, to represent the journey toward vulnerability.
- **Inner Critic in Writing:** Write a story from the perspective of your inner critic, exploring its critiques, protections, and transformation.

Journaling with Integration Intent

Journaling with Integration Intent is a focused approach to shadow work, chronicling your journey of accepting and merging specific shadow aspects with your conscious self.

Engaging in Journaling with Integration Intent:

1. **Designate Sections:** Create dedicated sections or chapters in your shadow work journal for each shadow aspect you're integrating. Label them clearly for reference.

2. **Initiate the Dialogue:** Begin each section by addressing the chosen shadow aspect. Start with a greeting, acknowledging your ongoing journey of integration.

3. **Reflect on the Journey:** Write about your experiences, thoughts, and emotions related to the shadow aspect. Reflect on moments of resistance, acceptance, and transformation.

4. **Acknowledge Progress:** Celebrate your progress in integrating the shadow aspect. Please describe how your relationship with it has evolved and influenced your life.

5. **Explore Transformations:** Share insights into the changes and transformations you've noticed since integrating this aspect. Discuss how it has enriched your self-awareness and relationships.

Examples of Journaling with Integration Intent:

Embracing Vulnerability: *"Dear Vulnerability, I've noticed a shift as I continue to embrace your presence. I'm no longer afraid of showing my authentic self, which has deepened my connections. Vulnerability has become a source of strength."*

Accepting Anger: *"Dear Anger, our journey has been challenging, but I understand your role. As I've accepted you, I'm more assertive and maintain healthier relationships. I've found a constructive outlet for my anger through art and physical activity."*

Daily Affirmations

Daily Affirmations are a powerful practice in shadow work, reinforcing the integration of your shadow aspects with your conscious self.

Engaging in Daily Affirmations:

1. **Set an Affirmation Ritual:** Dedicate a specific time daily for affirmations, either in the morning or before bedtime.

2. **Create Personalized Affirmations:** Craft affirmations in the present tense, positively phrased, and tailored to your unique journey of shadow integration.

3. **Repeat Regularly:** Say or write your affirmations daily, using them as a mantra during meditation. Repetition strengthens the message and deepens your connection.

4. **Feel the Affirmations:** Connect with the emotions evoked by the affirmations, embracing feelings of acceptance, wholeness, and self-love.

Examples of Daily Affirmations for Shadow Integration:

- **Embracing Vulnerability:** *"I wholeheartedly accept my vulnerability. It is a well-spring of authenticity and strength within me."*
- **Balancing Anger:** *"I harmoniously integrate my anger, transforming it into a force for positive change. I am at peace with my emotions."*
- **Honoring Imperfections:** *"I celebrate my imperfections as unique and beautiful facets of my being. I am beautifully human, flaws and all."*

Guided Meditation

Guided Meditation is a powerful tool for shadow work, using visualization to merge your conscious self with hidden aspects.

How to Do It:

1. **Engaging in Guided Meditation:**
   Choose Specific Meditations: Find guided sessions for shadow integration on apps, websites, or from experienced therapists.
   Create a Relaxing Space: Set up a quiet, comfortable space with calming elements.

2. **During the Meditation:**
   Follow Narration: Let the narrator guide you through a visualization, leading inner journeys to interact with concealed aspects.
   Visualize Integration: Imagine your conscious self merging harmoniously with shadow aspects, fostering unity and balance.
   Embrace Emotions: Notice and embrace feelings that arise, such as relief, acceptance, and increased self-awareness.

3. **Examples of Guided Meditation for Shadow Integration:**
   Embracing Vulnerability: Visualize encountering your vulnerable self, enveloped in a warm, accepting light for safety and acceptance.
   Balancing Anger: Meet inner anger, envisioning it as a powerful force for positive change, transforming into empowerment.
   Honoring Imperfections: Celebrate imperfections as unique facets contributing to your wholeness and authenticity.

Dream Analysis

Dream Analysis is crucial for shadow work, offering insights into your unconscious mind and revealing concealed aspects.

1. **Engaging in Dream Analysis:**
   Keep a Dream Journal: Document dreams vividly, including details, emotions, and symbols.
   Identify Patterns: Look for recurring themes, symbols, or emotions over time.
   Consult Resources: Use dream dictionaries and symbolism guides, or work with a therapist for interpretation.
   Reflect and Connect: Contemplate dream themes about waking life and the shadow aspects you're addressing.

2. **Integration Exploration:**
    Use Dreams for Integration: Explore how dream elements represent shadow aspects and integrate them consciously.
    Methods: Employ journaling, visualizations, or affirmations based on dream insights.

3. **Examples of Dream Analysis:**
    Vulnerability in Dreams: Repeated exposure or vulnerability dreams may signal concealed aspects seeking recognition. Analyze to embrace vulnerability consciously.
    Anger-Related Dreams: Frequent anger or conflict dreams reveal suppressed emotions. Analyze to uncover sources and integrate anger constructively.
    Imperfections in Dreams: Dreams featuring flaws suggest a longing to accept imperfections in waking life. Analyze to appreciate your humanity.

Mindfulness Practices: Anchoring in the Present Moment

Mindfulness practices are crucial tools in shadow work, helping you observe thoughts, emotions, and concealed aspects without judgment. Here's a concise breakdown:

1. **Meditation:**
    Focus: Regular meditation cultivates non-judgmental awareness, especially during breath-focused sessions.
    Observation: Notice when your mind drifts to shadow-related thoughts, fostering detachment from concealed qualities.

2. **Body Scan:**
    Systematic Attention: Direct focus to different body parts, noting sensations and tensions.
    Awareness: Enhances observation of physical discomfort linked to shadow aspects.

3. **Mindful Walking:**
    Deliberate Movement: Slow, deliberate walking encourages attention to each step and bodily sensations.
    Observation: Notice thoughts and emotions related to shadow aspects, promoting non-judgmental observation.

4. **Observing Thoughts:**
    Cloud Analogy: View thoughts as passing clouds, fostering non-attachment.
    Shadow Thoughts: Observe shadow-related thoughts without getting entangled in their narratives.

5. **Emotional Awareness:**
    Recognize Emotions: Heightens awareness of surface emotions related to shadow aspects.
    Exploration: Enables sitting with emotions, exploring origins without reactive responses.

6. **Mindful Eating:**
    Sensory Focus: Concentrate on the sensory experience of eating.

Reveal Relationships: Exposes emotional ties between food and concealed qualities, promoting healthier coping.

7. **Observing Reactions:**
External Triggers: Notice reactions to external events triggering shadow aspects.
Conscious Choice: Observe emotional and behavioral responses, choosing compassionate reactions.

Through mindfulness, approach concealed qualities with curiosity and compassion, facilitating their integration into your conscious self.

Inner Child Work

Inner child work is a potent technique in shadow work, involving connecting with your younger self to explore past experiences.

Process of Inner Child Work:

1. **Visualization:** Connect with your inner child through guided visualization or meditation, meeting them at a significant age.

2. **Dialogue:** Compassionate dialogue with your inner child, exploring feelings, needs, and past events.

3. **Reparenting:** Offer love, care, and support to your inner child, reparenting as a nurturing caregiver.

4. **Integration:** Heal and nurture your inner child, integrating insights into your adult self for conscious choices and self-compassion.

Integration is an ongoing process that leads to wholeness and authenticity as you merge your shadow aspects with your conscious self.

Examples of Inner Child Work:

1. **Vulnerability Exploration:** Revisit memories of your inner child feeling exposed to understand current struggles with vulnerability.

2. **Inner Critic Origins:** Explore messages and criticisms received by your inner child, shaping the development of your inner critic.

3. **Fear and Insecurities:** Identify early experiences instilling fears in your younger self, offering comfort and reassurance for healing.

4. **Empowerment and Self-Worth:** Explore memories of disempowerment, providing empowerment and self-worth to your inner child.

Inner Dialogue Journal

Instructions:

Use this page to document your inner dialogues with different shadow aspects. Keep a record of your conversations, insights, and the progress you make toward shadow integration.

Shadow Aspect: [Specify the shadow aspect you are engaging with] _____

_____

_____

_____

_____

_____

_____

Date: _____

Conversation Highlights: [List key points, revelations, or emotions discussed during the dialogue] _____

_____

_____

_____

_____

Integration Action Plan: [Detail your plan for integrating the insights from this dialogue into your conscious self] _____

_____

_____

_____

_____

_____

_____

Soul Collage

Creative Expression

Inner Child Work

Instructions:

Engaging in inner child work is a powerful technique in shadow work. This practice involves connecting with your inner child, the younger version of yourself, to explore memories and experiences from their perspective. It allows you to access insights into the origins of your concealed qualities and work toward their integration.

Inner Child Connection:

Age of Inner Child: [Specify the age of your inner child that you intend to connect with.]

Memories to Explore: [List specific memories or experiences from your past that you want to explore during this inner child work.]

Feelings and Emotions: [Describe the feelings and emotions associated with your inner child's experiences. How did they feel during those moments?]

Integration Journey:

Insights and Learnings: [Share any insights or learnings gained from connecting with your inner child. What have you discovered about the origins of your concealed qualities?]

Healing and Compassion: [Describe how you provided healing and compassion to your inner child during this process. How did this impact your relationship with your concealed qualities?]

Transformation — The Culmination of Shadow Work

Transformation commences with acknowledging concealed qualities, parts of the self veiled by fear, guilt, and shame. This self-awareness ignites a transformative process akin to alchemy.

As one delves into their inner world, they confront suppressed emotions and inner demons, navigating past traumas and assessing the profound impact of early life experiences. Through this journey, the chains binding these shadow aspects are broken, allowing them to emerge into the light.

The alchemical transformation within is not merely about banishing the shadow but integrating its wisdom into the conscious self. It leads to increased authenticity, compassion, and resilience. The once critical inner voice is replaced by a more supportive one, and the fear and insecurity that once hindered personal growth now serve as catalysts for positive change.

The effects of this transformation extend beyond the internal realm, impacting external realities. By shedding self-sabotaging behaviors, cultivating self-worth, and embracing vulnerability, relationships, work, and life, in general, are enriched.

In shadow work, transformation is about achieving balance and authenticity by embracing both light and dark aspects of the self. The journey is continuous, akin to tending to a garden, requiring ongoing self-reflection and nurturing to achieve an authentic and fulfilled existence. In this process, the self undergoes a profound and continual transformation, reflecting the essence while adapting to evolving layers. The result is a more genuine and fulfilled existence, a testament to the harmonious integration of light and shadow within the self.

Chapter 5
Journaling Your Shadows

The power of journaling lies in providing a non-judgmental space to record and process encounters with shadow aspects. It clarifies emotions, allowing deep exploration of triggers and patterns related to concealed qualities. Consistent journaling aids in recognizing these patterns, leading to a powerful affirmation of integration. Sections dedicated to specific shadow qualities can include affirmations, reinforcing commitment to embracing and harmoniously integrating these aspects into the conscious self for peace and acceptance.

Establishing a Journaling Routine

Select a journal format that suits your lifestyle — traditional, digital, or computer-based. Whether you choose to journal at the beginning or end of each day, regularity helps track your progress. Integrate shadow work prompts and exercises, exploring emotions triggered by your inner critic or practicing self-compassion. Regularly review entries to reflect on your journey, celebrate growth, and acknowledge progress in embracing concealed qualities.

Journal Prompts for Shadow Work

Journal prompts are indispensable tools in shadow work, providing guidance and structure for your inner exploration. These prompts are designed to evoke thoughtful self-reflection, helping you navigate the concealed qualities of your psyche.

Exploring Childhood Memories:
Unlocking the Origins of Your Shadows

Explore childhood memories to uncover the origins of your shadows — a crucial aspect of shadow work. Your formative years shape beliefs, behaviors, and hidden qualities. These memories provide vital clues about when and why certain aspects became concealed, offering a deeper understanding.

Recognize recurring patterns and experiences in childhood memories that influence your adult life. Connecting with the emotional underpinnings of concealed qualities is essential. Childhood memories may hold traumatic experiences contributing to shadow formation, a critical step in healing past wounds.

Examples include exploring moments of suppressed anger, identifying childhood vulnerabilities, revisiting criticism influencing your inner critic, and understanding how early expectations formed shadows like perfectionism.

Uncovering Core Beliefs

Get to the core of your concealed qualities by uncovering profoundly ingrained beliefs. These beliefs, shaped by past experiences, underlie your behaviors and reactions. Discovering core beliefs opens the door to understanding behavioral patterns, facilitating transformation, and providing an opportunity for reframing.

Examples:

- **Perfectionism:** Uncover the belief, *"I am only worthy if I'm perfect,"* possibly rooted in conditional praise or love during early experiences.
- **People-Pleasing:** Explore the core belief, *"I am only valuable when I make others happy,"* often tied to childhood experiences where self-worth depended on pleasing others.
- **Inner Critic:** Expose beliefs like *"I am flawed and unlovable,"* stemming from critical messages in childhood.
- **Self-Worth Issues:** Struggling with self-worth may reveal beliefs like *"I am not deserving of love or respect,"* shaped by early experiences of rejection or neglect.

Healing Trauma

Coping mechanisms stemming from trauma can transform into shadow aspects, emphasizing the importance of healing trauma to address its root causes.

Examples of Healing Trauma:

1. **Childhood Abuse:** Address emotional scars and fears, confronting shadow aspects like the inner critic or self-worth issues.
2. **Loss and Grief:** Heal trauma related to losses, allowing the processing of grief and addressing shadow aspects like repressed emotions or fear of abandonment.
3. **PTSD (Post-Traumatic Stress Disorder):** Employ therapies to reduce the impact of traumatic memories, addressing shadow aspects linked to emotional triggers and reactivity.
4. **Attachment Trauma:** Work through trauma related to attachment issues, contributing to shadow aspects like fear of intimacy or self-reliance.

Facing Fears and Insecurities

Address concealed qualities from unresolved emotional challenges by facing fears and insecurities, recognizing them as catalysts for shadow aspects. Confrontation encourages self-exploration, leading to a deeper understanding of shadows and empowering you to take charge.

Examples include initiating conversations to confront the fear of rejection or expressing opinions in group settings to address people-pleasing tendencies.

Identifying Patterns

Identifying patterns is crucial in shadow work, revealing recurrent behaviors, thoughts, and emotions that are key to understanding concealed qualities. These patterns serve as a blueprint for shadows, shedding light on their motivations and origins, enhancing self-awareness, and providing insights. Once recognized, patterns can be transformed, empowering individuals to make conscious choices and foster personal growth.

Examples include

- patterns of procrastination indicating underlying shadow aspects like self-doubt, fear of failure, or perfectionism;
- patterns of people-pleasing revealing issues related to low self-worth or fear of rejection;

- patterns of conflict avoidance linked to shadow aspects associated with fear of anger or abandonment, and recurring self-criticism patterns tied to inner critic or low self-esteem shadow aspects.

Forgiving and Letting Go

Forgiveness is key for emotional freedom and shadow integration, releasing emotional burdens tied to past hurts and resentments. Holding onto these can contribute to shadow aspects such as anger, bitterness, and emotional reactivity. It's an act of self-compassion, fostering self-acceptance and acknowledging imperfections for effective shadow integration.

Examples include:

- forgiving a past betrayal to address trust issues and emotional guardedness,
- practicing self-forgiveness to address self-criticism and low self-esteem,
- releasing anger to deal with reactivity and emotional intensity, and
- accepting imperfections to address perfectionism or the inner critic.

Cultivating Self-Compassion

Self-compassion, treating oneself with kindness and understanding, is a powerful tool for addressing concealed qualities developed in response to self-criticism and blame. It counters self-criticism, fueling shadowy aspects like the inner critic and low self-esteem, fostering emotional healing related to past wounds. Self-compassion encourages self-acceptance, a critical aspect of shadow integration, by creating an environment for recognition and acceptance.

Examples:

- **Offering Self-Comfort:** provide self-comfort instead of criticism after a mistake.
- **Treating Oneself as a Friend:** Approach challenging situations with the kindness you would offer a friend.
- **Acknowledging Painful Emotions**: Face painful emotions with self-kindness.
- **Prioritizing Self-Care:** Engage in self-care activities to promote self-acceptance and self-worth.

Reconnecting with Your Inner Child

This process serves as a means to address childhood wounds, such as neglect, abandonment, or trauma, which is essential for shadow integration. Moreover, it facilitates the rekindling of joy, curiosity, and playfulness, as your inner child embodies these qualities. Reconnecting with this part of yourself infuses life with wonder and creativity. This practice also encourages empathy and self-nurturing by extending the same care and understanding you would offer to a child. Examples of reconnecting with your inner child include:

- engaging in playful activities you enjoyed as a child,
- writing a comforting letter to your younger self,
- revisiting childhood photos and memories to evoke a sense of nostalgia and
- embracing imaginary play to tap into your creative and imaginative aspects.

Chapter 6
Beyond Shadow Work

Shadow work, though transformative, is not the end of your journey but a significant milestone on a path of lifelong self-discovery. This is a Journey Without End.

The culmination of shadow work signifies liberation from past burdens and opens the door to limitless self-discovery. It's a journey without defined boundaries, guided by the compass of your true self.

Beyond shadow work, individuals naturally gravitate toward self-evolution. They may delve deeper into unexplored passions, nurture existing talents, or even embark on new life paths. Engage in continuous learning, whether through courses, workshops, or literature that align with your evolving interests.

The heightened emotional awareness developed during shadow work remains a constant ally. It involves maintaining a deep connection with your feelings, recognizing emotional triggers, and responding mindfully.

After shadow work, relationships tend to deepen. Improved communication, enhanced empathy, and a profound self-understanding contribute to more authentic and meaningful connections with loved ones.

Let this become a part of your life, not a short-term task:

1. Mindfulness Practice
2. Journaling
3. Setting Personal Goals
4. Self-Compassion
5. Seeking New Experiences

Conclusion

Beyond shadow work, sustaining personal growth is not a choice but an inherent aspect of your journey. It ensures that you continue to evolve, grow, and deepen your understanding of yourself and the world. Embrace new experiences, practice self-compassion, and set personal goals as you embark on an unending journey of self-discovery and personal development. The path unfolds infinitely, guided by your inner truth.

In the pages of this book, we've embarked on a profound journey through the intricate realms of self-discovery, delving into the depths of our shadow selves. Shadow work has unveiled the transformative power of embracing our hidden aspects and integrating them into our conscious being.

We've explored the significance of understanding our inner shadows, the archetypes that shape us, and the impact of shadows on our relationships. We've delved into the four stages of shadow work, equipping you with a toolkit of techniques and exercises to guide your personal growth.

But the journey doesn't end here. It's a lifelong quest, a continuous evolution. As you move forward, remember that you are your healer and guide. Your shadows are not to be feared but embraced, for they hold the key to your highest potential.

Now that you have the proper knowledge, put it into practice. Begin your journey of self-discovery and shadow work. Take the first step towards a more integrated and authentic you. If this book has been helpful in your quest, please leave a review on Amazon. Your feedback will help others on their path to wholeness.

Your Personal

Shadow Work Journey

Day 1
Exploring Your Inner Landscape

Date _____

The first day of your 28-day job shadow plan is all about self-exploration. Before you embark on shadow work, it's crucial to understand your current emotional and mental landscape. This day will set the foundation for the entire journey by helping you become more self-aware.

Outcome:

By the end of Day 1, you will have a clearer understanding of your current emotional state, thoughts, and behaviors. This self-awareness will serve as a starting point for identifying and working with your shadows.

Exercises:

Mood and Emotion Tracking: Throughout the day, pay close attention to your moods and emotions. You can use a journal to record how you feel at different times. Be as specific as possible. For example, *"9:00 AM — Felt anxious while preparing for work."*

Self-Reflection: Take time in the evening to reflect on your day. Consider the situations or events that triggered specific emotions. Try to identify any recurring thought patterns or behaviors.

Examples:

Mood and Emotion Tracking: You may notice that you felt irritable when dealing with a difficult coworker, or you experienced joy when you achieved a personal goal.

Self-Reflection: During self-reflection, you might realize that your irritation with your coworker is related to unresolved past experiences of feeling unheard or disrespected. This is a sign that there might be a shadow aspect associated with this trigger.

Remember:

The goal of Day 1 is to establish self-awareness. It's the first step in recognizing your shadows and how they influence your thoughts and emotions. This foundation will be essential as you progress through the 28-day job shadow plan.

Mood and Emotion Tracking

Mood Scale: _____
What did I do? _____

_____
_____
_____
_____
_____
_____
_____
_____

How do I feel? _____

_____
_____
_____
_____
_____
_____
_____

Why did I feel this? _____

_____
_____
_____
_____
_____
_____
_____

Reflection Space

Day 2
Exploring Archetypes

Date _____

Today, it uses archetypes to deepen your understanding of shadow aspects. Archetypes are universal symbols in the collective unconscious representing facets of the human experience. Identifying these in your life provides insights into concealed qualities and motivations.

By the end of the day, you'll better understand how archetypes relate to your shadow work, identifying prominent ones and their connection to hidden qualities, aiding in further integration.

Exercises:

1. **Archetype Identification:**
   Research archetypes like the Hero, Mother, Sage, and Shadow.
   Reflect in a journal on which archetypes resonate with you and when they've been prevalent.

2. **Archetypal Dream Analysis:**
   Keep a dream journal for a few nights, identifying recurring archetypes or symbols. Reflect on what these symbols reveal about concealed qualities.

3. **Archetypal Writing:**
   Write a short story incorporating identified archetypes, fictional or inspired by life. Analyze the story for insights into concealed qualities.

Examples:

1. **Archetype Identification:**
   Discovering a solid connection to the Wanderer archetype may lead to exploring its prevalence in your life and its relation to shadow aspects.

2. **Archetypal Dream Analysis:**
   A recurring Warrior archetype in dreams may signify a constant battle, providing insights into internal struggles.

3. **Archetypal Writing:**
   Creating a story personifying the Lover and Trickster archetypes can reveal interactions between desires and playful aspects, shedding light on concealed qualities.

Remember: Exploring archetypes deepens understanding of shadow aspects, providing valuable insights into concealed qualities and motivations.

Archetype Identification

Archetype	Meaning	Situations or Periods Where Prevalent

Archetypal Dream Analysis

Dream Description and Symbols	Recurring Archetypes or Symbols	Reflection on Concealed Qualities

Archetypal Writing

Title: [Title of Your Story]

Archetypes: [List the archetypes you're incorporating in your story]

Story or Narrative:

[Write your short story or narrative here. This can be a fictional tale or a reflection on a real-life experience. Use the chosen archetypes to inspire your story.]

Analysis:

[After writing your story, analyze it to understand how the chosen archetypes manifest and interact within the narrative.]

Archetype 1: [Discuss how this archetype is represented in the story, the role it plays, and any hidden qualities it might reveal.]

Archetype 2: [Discuss the representation, role, and insights associated with the second archetype.]

[Continue this pattern for each archetype you've used in your story.]

Insights:

[Summarize the insights you've gained from the story. Reflect on how the archetypes and their interactions shed light on your concealed qualities.]

This exercise can provide a deep understanding of your hidden aspects through the creative exploration of archetypal themes in your writing.

Your Story

Day 3
Unveiling Your Inner Critic

Date _____

On the third day, we'll delve into one of the most common shadow aspects: the inner critic. This internal voice can be harsh and critical, often holding you back from your full potential. Today's focus is on identifying and understanding your inner critic.

Outcome:

By the end of Day 3, you will have a clearer awareness of your inner critic's presence and how it influences your thoughts and behaviors. This awareness is the initial step in integrating this shadow aspect.

Exercises:

Self-Reflection: Throughout the day, pay attention to moments when your inner critic emerges. Note the specific situations, thoughts, and self-critical language it uses. For example, *"11:30 AM — Inner critic appeared when I made a mistake at work."*

Inner Critic Journaling: In the evening, dedicate a journal entry to your inner critic. Write down the critical thoughts you observed during the day. Challenge these thoughts with self-compassionate responses.

Affirmation: In addition to the exercises, use affirmations to counteract your inner critic's negative self-talk. Affirmations are positive statements that can help shift your mindset.

Examples:

Self-Reflection: You might notice that your inner critic appears when you receive feedback on a project at work. It tells you that you're not good enough and that everyone is better than you.

Inner Critic Journaling: You write down, *"My inner critic tells me I'm not good enough at work. I challenge this thought by reminding myself that I'm continually learning and improving. Mistakes are part of the growth process."*

Remember:

Day 3 focuses on one specific shadow aspect, the inner critic. As you observe and journal about its influence on your thoughts and feelings, you'll begin the process of understanding and ultimately integrating this aspect of your shadow.

Self-Reflection: Unveiling Your Inner Critic

Situation/Trigger	Inner Critic Thoughts	Self-Compassionate Response

Affirmations

Here are 20 affirmations specifically designed to counteract the negative self-talk of the inner critic:

I release self-doubt and embrace self-confidence.

I am kind and gentle with myself.

I let go of perfectionism and accept my imperfections.

I trust in my abilities and inner wisdom.

I am free from the grip of my inner critic.

I replace self-criticism with self-compassion.

I am deserving of love and acceptance.

I choose to focus on my strengths and accomplishments.

I release the need for external validation.

I believe in my own worth and value.

I am my own biggest supporter and cheerleader.

I silence the inner critic's negative chatter.

I am resilient and can handle any challenge.

I embrace my mistakes as opportunities for growth.

I let go of comparing myself to others.

I am enough just as I am.

I am proud of my unique qualities and quirks.

I replace fear with faith in myself.

I am the master of my thoughts and emotions.

I am free to be authentically me.

Choose the affirmations that resonate with you and use them regularly to counter the influence of your inner critic and promote self-compassion and self-acceptance.

Day 4
Connecting with Your Inner Child

Date _____

We'll explore your inner child, an essential aspect of your shadow. Your inner child holds memories, emotions, and experiences from your past that continue to shape your present. Today, the focus is on understanding, connecting with, and healing this inner aspect.

Outcome:

By the end of Day 4, you will have established a deeper connection with your inner child, allowing you to access and work through past experiences that influence your current emotions and behaviors. This connection is vital for healing and integrating this aspect of your shadow.

Exercises:

Inner Child Visualization: Find a quiet, comfortable space and close your eyes. Visualize yourself as a child, around 5–7 years old. Imagine the environment you grew up in and the experiences you had. Try to evoke the feelings of your inner child. What does your inner child need or want to express? Take notes afterward.

Letter to Your Inner Child: Write a letter to your inner child, offering love, understanding, and reassurance. You can start with, "Dear [Your Name]'s Inner Child, I want you to know..."

Examples:

Inner Child Visualization: During the visualization, you might see yourself as a young child playing in your childhood home. You may feel a sense of nostalgia and recall moments of joy and innocence.

Letter to Your Inner Child: In your letter, you may express compassion for the pain or challenges your inner child experienced, and offer words of comfort and support. For example, "I want you to know that I am here for you, and I will protect and care for you."

Remember:

Day 4 focuses on understanding and connecting with your inner child, a critical aspect of your shadow. This connection will help you explore and heal past experiences that influence your present emotions and behaviors. It's a compassionate step toward integrating this aspect of your shadow.

Inner Child Visualization Worksheet

Setting	Emotions	Messages or Insights

Inner Child Letter Template

[Your Name]'s Inner Child Letter

[Date: _____]

Dear [Your Name]'s Inner Child,

I want you to know that I am here for you. I understand that you carry feelings, memories, and needs from our past, and I'm committed to providing the love and support you need.

Acknowledging Your Feelings:

I know that there have been times when you felt [describe emotions or feelings from your past, e.g., scared, lonely, unloved]. I want you to know that it's okay to feel this way. Your feelings are valid, and I'm here to listen.

Meeting Your Needs:

I am dedicated to meeting your needs, just as any caring and loving guardian would. Your needs matter to me. What can I do to make you feel safe, loved, and nurtured? Please tell me your needs, and I will do my best to fulfill them.

Offering Reassurance:

You are not alone, and you are not to blame for anything that happened in the past. I am here to protect and care for you. Together, we can heal and grow stronger.

Forgiveness and Love:

I want you to know that I forgive any mistakes or hurts from the past. I forgive [mention any specific situations, people, or events]. It's time to release the burdens of the past and replace them with love and compassion.

Moving Forward:

As we work together to heal and integrate, I promise to be patient and kind with you. We are a team, and I am committed to your well-being.

Closing Words:

You are a precious part of who I am, and I embrace you with open arms and an open heart. We are in this journey together, and I promise to protect, love, and nurture you as you deserve.

With love and understanding,

[Your Name]

Feel free to use this template as a starting point for your inner child letters. Personalize it as you see fit and let it serve as a tool to connect with and provide reassurance to your inner child during your shadow work.

Day 5
Nurturing Your Inner Child

Date _____

Continuing our journey of self-discovery and inner child work, Day 5 is all about nurturing and caring for the needs and desires of your inner child. Your inner child holds the key to many unmet longings from the past, and today is an opportunity to address those needs with love and compassion.

Outcome:

By the end of Day 5, you will have a deeper understanding of your inner child's needs and desires. You will also develop positive affirmations to nurture and support your inner child. In addition, you will create a Memory Map that helps you recognize significant childhood memories and the emotions associated with them.

Exercises:

Memory Map: Use the provided chart to draw or list significant childhood memories that arise during your inner child visualization. In each section, make note of the emotions you felt during those memories. This exercise will help you gain clarity about your inner child's past experiences.

Needs and Desires Sheet: Complete the sheet by listing the needs and desires of your inner child. These could include emotional needs, such as feeling loved and safe, as well as desires like playfulness, creativity, and adventure. Recognizing these needs is an essential step in providing the care your inner child requires.

Affirmations for Inner Child: Use the sheet to create affirmations that specifically address your inner child's needs and offer comfort and support. For example, *"I nurture my inner child with love and understanding. My inner child is safe and cherished."*

Examples:

Memory Map: You may recall a childhood memory of building a sandcastle on the beach. You might note that you felt joyful and carefree during that memory.

Needs and Desires Sheet: Your inner child's needs and desires might include feeling heard and valued, experiencing moments of pure joy and laughter, and receiving comfort during times of fear.

Affirmations for Inner Child: Create affirmations that reflect your inner child's needs and your commitment to fulfilling them. For instance, *"I provide my inner child with the safety and love they deserve."*

Remember:

Day 5 is a vital continuation of your inner child work. It allows you to explore your inner child's past, acknowledge their needs and desires, and develop affirmations to nurture and support them throughout your shadow work journey.

Memory Map: My Inner Child's Journey

Memory Description	Emotions Felt

Needs and Desires Sheet for My Inner Child

Emotional Needs:

- To feel loved and cherished.
- To feel safe and secure.
- To feel heard and understood.
- To experience joy and playfulness.
- To express creativity and imagination.
- To have a sense of belonging and connection.
- To feel free to explore and learn.

Desires:

- To have moments of pure joy and laughter.
- To engage in creative and imaginative activities.
- To play and have fun without worry.
- To feel a sense of adventure and exploration.
- To receive comfort and reassurance during moments of fear.
- To be encouraged and supported in pursuing interests.
- To be surrounded by positive role models and nurturing figures.

Unmet Needs:

- To have past fears and insecurities acknowledged.
- To receive validation for feelings and experiences.
- To heal from past emotional wounds.
- To be free from any burdens or responsibilities that were too heavy for a child.

Healing Desires:

- To receive self-compassion and self-love.
- To provide nurturing and care to the inner child.
- To create a safe and loving environment for the inner child.
- To fulfill unmet needs through self-compassion and self-care.

Feel free to use this template to identify and explore the needs, desires, unmet needs, and healing desires of your inner child. This process can guide you in nurturing and supporting your inner child throughout your shadow work journey.

Affirmations for Inner Child

Here are 20 affirmations designed to nurture and support your inner child:

My inner child is a cherished part of who I am, and I embrace them with love and understanding.

I offer my inner child the love and compassion they deserve.

My inner child is safe and protected, and I provide a secure and nurturing space for them.

I release the burdens of the past from my inner child and fill their heart with joy and playfulness.

I listen to my inner child's needs and desires and work to fulfill them with love.

My inner child is free to explore, create, and imagine without fear or judgment.

I provide comfort and reassurance to my inner child during moments of fear or insecurity.

My inner child is worthy of love, happiness, and a carefree spirit.

I offer my inner child moments of pure joy and laughter, allowing them to experience life's beauty.

I release the pain of the past and replace it with self-compassion and self-love for my inner child.

My inner child's dreams and desires are valid, and I support them in pursuing what brings them fulfillment.

I create a loving and nurturing environment where my inner child can heal and thrive.

I embrace the innocence and curiosity of my inner child, allowing them to be their authentic self.

My inner child is a source of strength and resilience, and I honor their presence in my life.

I acknowledge the past wounds of my inner child and work to heal and mend those emotional scars.

I encourage my inner child to express their creativity, imagination, and unique talents.

My inner child is a beacon of light within me, guiding me to a life filled with love and happiness.

I am committed to nurturing and supporting my inner child in all aspects of life.

My inner child is a cherished companion on my journey, and I embrace them with an open heart.

I recognize that my inner child holds the key to my authentic self, and I lovingly connect with them, fostering inner peace and wholeness.

Feel free to select the affirmations that resonate most with you and your inner child, and use them to provide loving care and support throughout your shadow work journey.

Day 6
Embracing Inner Child Creativity

Date _____

Today's focus is on tapping into your inner child's creativity and self-expression. By engaging in creative activities, you'll connect with your inner child's emotions and experiences on a deeper level. This day encourages exploration through coloring, art, and self-reflection.

Outcome:

At the end of the day, you'll have a better understanding of your inner child's creative desires and emotional expression. You'll also have tangible expressions of your inner child's world through coloring, art, and a collage.

Exercises:

Inner Child Art Expression: If you enjoy drawing or painting, express your inner child's emotions and experiences through art. Let your inner child guide your creative process. For instance, if your inner child feels adventurous, create a painting of an imaginative adventure.

Collage Space: Create a collage representing your inner child's world and experiences. Use images, words, and symbols that connect with your inner child's desires and feelings. For example, if your inner child longs for freedom, include images of open skies or soaring birds.

Guided Questionnaire: Use the guided questionnaire to delve deeper into your inner child's feelings and experiences.

Remember:

These exercises are not about producing perfect art but about connecting with your inner child's creative and emotional world. Use this day to nurture and celebrate your inner child's creativity.

Inner Child Art

Collage Sace

Inner Child Exploration Questionnaire

1. Creative Desires:
— What creative activities did your inner child enjoy the most during your childhood?

— Are there any artistic interests or talents your inner child wishes to explore now?

2. Emotional Expression:
— How does your inner child feel when they engage in creative expression?

— Are there specific emotions your inner child wants to express through art or other creative outlets?

3. Childhood Memories:
— Can you recall any significant childhood memories related to creativity or art?

— How did these memories make your inner child feel at the time?

4. Dreams and Fantasies:
— Did your inner child have any dreams or fantasies related to art or creativity?

— What can you do to make those dreams a reality for your inner child now?

5. Emotional Impact:

— How does engaging in creative activities make your inner child feel today?

— Are there any emotional obstacles or fears your inner child faces when expressing themselves creatively?

6. Support and Nurturing:

— Reflect on the support your inner child received (or lacked) in pursuing creative interests.

— How can you provide the support and nurturing your inner child needs to explore their creative side now?

7. Creative Vision:

— Ask your inner child what kind of creative world they envision.

— How can you bring elements of that vision into your current creative pursuits?

8. Release and Healing:

— Explore whether creative activities can serve as a means for your inner child to release past pain or emotional wounds.

— What steps can you take to create a healing space for your inner child's creative expression?

9. Unfulfilled Desires:

— Are there creative desires your inner child had but never had the chance to fulfill?

— How can you work towards fulfilling those desires now?

10. Future Nurturing:

— Reflect on how you can continue nurturing and supporting your inner child's creativity as you move forward in your shadow work journey.

Use this guided questionnaire to engage in self-reflection and gain a deeper understanding of your inner child's creative desires and emotional needs. It can be a valuable tool for nurturing and celebrating your inner child's creativity.

Day 7
Confronting Your Inner Saboteur

Date _____

This critical aspect often undermines your progress and prevents you from reaching your full potential. In the next few days, we'll delve deep into identifying, understanding, and ultimately transforming this self-sabotaging pattern.

Outcome:

By the end of these three days, you'll have a comprehensive understanding of your inner saboteur, including its triggers, the impact it has on your life, and strategies to overcome its influence. Confronting your inner saboteur is an essential step toward personal growth and breaking free from self-destructive patterns.

Exercises:

Inner Saboteur Identification: Reflect on previous situations where your inner saboteur emerged. Make a list of these instances, noting the thoughts, emotions, and behaviors that triggered self-sabotage.

Negative Self-Talk Awareness: Throughout the day, pay close attention to moments when you engage in negative self-talk. Record specific situations, thoughts, and the language you use when undermining yourself.

Triggers Exploration: Identify common triggers that activate your inner saboteur. These triggers could be specific situations, people, or emotions. Create a list to better understand what sets it in motion.

Examples:

Inner Saboteur Identification Example: Recall a time when you self-sabotaged a project due to self-doubt and fear of failure. Note the thoughts and emotions that led to this behavior.

Negative Self-Talk Awareness Example: Document instances during the day when negative self-talk took control. For instance, if you doubted your abilities at work, record this occurrence.

Triggers Exploration Example: List situations or events that commonly lead to self-sabotage. These could include public speaking, taking risks, or facing criticism. Document what you discover during your exploration.

Remember:

Recognizing and understanding this aspect of yourself is a vital step toward growth and self-transformation. Be patient and compassionate with yourself as you delve into this journey of self-discovery.

Inner Saboteur Identification

Situation/Trigger: [Describe the situation or trigger that led to your inner saboteur emerging.] _____

_____

_____

What Did Your Inner Saboteur Say?: [Write down the negative self-talk, self-doubt, or critical thoughts your inner saboteur used in this situation. _____

_____

_____

Emotions You Felt: [List the emotions you experienced during this instance.] ____

_____

_____

Why Do You Think Your Inner Saboteur Reacted This Way?: [Reflect on the possible reasons your inner saboteur emerged during this situation.] _____

_____

_____

Impact on Your Actions/Decisions: [Describe how your inner saboteur's presence influenced your actions or decisions in this situation.] _____

_____

_____

Self-Compassionate Response: [Write down a self-compassionate and understanding response to your inner saboteur's thoughts.] _____

_____

_____

Negative Self-Talk Awareness

Situation/Event Leading to Negative Self-Talk	Negative Thoughts/ Inner Dialogue	Self-Critical Language Used

Triggers Exploration

Specific Trigger	Emotions/Reactions	Self-Sabotage Patterns

Day 8
Confronting Your Inner Saboteur (Part 2)

Date _____

Today, we continue our exploration of this self-sabotaging aspect and delve deeper into understanding its influence and finding strategies to overcome it.

Outcome:

By the end of these three days, you'll have a comprehensive understanding of your inner saboteur. You'll identify its triggers, recognize the impact it has on your life, and develop effective strategies to overcome its influence. Confronting your inner saboteur is a significant step toward personal growth and breaking free from self-destructive patterns.

Exercises:

Self-Sabotage Journal: Dedicate a section in your journal to self-sabotage. Record moments when you've undermined your own progress, and reflect on the patterns you observe.

Positive Affirmations: Create positive affirmations that counteract the negative self-talk used by your inner saboteur. Repeat these affirmations throughout the day.

Examples:

Self-Sabotage Journal Example: Recall instances where your inner saboteur affected your personal or professional life. Note down the situations, thoughts, emotions, and behaviors you observed.

Positive Affirmations Example: Develop affirmations that counteract your inner saboteur's negative influence. For instance, create an affirmation like, "I believe in my abilities, and I deserve success."

Remember:

Confronting your inner saboteur is a multi-day journey. Stay committed and compassionate with yourself as you work to understand and transform this self-sabotaging aspect. The insights gained during these days will significantly contribute to your personal growth and empowerment.

Self-Sabotage Journal

Situation/Event Leading to Self-Sabotage	Thoughts/Inner Dialogue	Emotions/ Feelings	Self-Sabotaging Behaviors

Use this chart to track instances when your inner saboteur emerges, the thoughts and emotions associated with it, and the self-sabotaging behaviors it leads to. This will help you gain a deeper understanding of this aspect and its patterns.

Affirmations

Here are 20 positive affirmations to counteract the influence of your inner saboteur:

I believe in my abilities and trust myself.

I deserve success and happiness in my life.

I am resilient and can overcome any challenges.

I release self-doubt and embrace self-confidence.

I am capable of achieving my goals and dreams.

I am in control of my thoughts and emotions.

I choose self-compassion over self-criticism.

I am worthy of love, both from myself and others.

I let go of fear and embrace courage.

I am a work in progress, and that's perfectly okay.

I replace negative self-talk with positive affirmations.

I trust the journey of personal growth.

I am not defined by my past mistakes.

I am open to learning and growing every day.

I release the need for perfection and embrace progress.

I am the creator of my own reality.

I am kind to myself in times of setbacks.

I choose empowerment over self-sabotage.

I celebrate my unique qualities and strengths.

I am the master of my inner world and my destiny.

Repeat these affirmations regularly to help shift your mindset and combat the influence of your inner saboteur.

Day 9
Confronting Your Inner Saboteur (Part 3)

Date _____

Today, we continue our exploration, focusing on strategies to overcome its influence and empower yourself to break free from self-destructive patterns.

Outcome:

By the end of these three days, you will have gained a comprehensive understanding of your inner saboteur, including its triggers, the impact it has on your life, and strategies to overcome its influence. Confronting your inner saboteur is a significant step toward personal growth and empowerment.

Exercises:

Empowerment Action Plan: Create a plan that outlines specific actions you can take to counteract your inner saboteur's influence. Identify strategies to boost your self-esteem and self-confidence.

Positive Visualization: Spend some time visualizing yourself successfully achieving your goals. Imagine the positive outcomes, and feel the emotions associated with your success.

Examples:

Empowerment Action Plan Example: Develop a plan that includes actions such as setting achievable goals, practicing positive self-talk, seeking support from others, and celebrating your successes, no matter how small.

Positive Visualization Example: Visualize a situation where your inner saboteur typically holds you back. Picture yourself confidently navigating this situation, achieving success, and feeling a sense of accomplishment.

Remember:

Confronting your inner saboteur is an essential journey that requires ongoing self-awareness and empowerment. The insights and strategies gained during these three days will contribute significantly to your personal growth and ability to overcome self-sabotage. Stay committed to your empowerment and well-being.

Set Achievable Goals

Long-term Goal:

Smaller, Achievable Steps

Step 1:

Deadline:

How I'll Celebrate:

Step 2:

Deadline:

How I'll Celebrate:

Step 3:

Deadline:

How I'll Celebrate:

Tracking Progress:

Step	Date Completed	Percentage Achieved

Self-Compassionate Self-Talk. Mirror Mork

Replace self-criticism with self-compassionate self-talk. Instead of harshly criticizing yourself, remind yourself that making mistakes is an opportunity for growth.

Find a quiet and comfortable space. Stand in front of the mirror and make eye contact with yourself, recognizing the deep connection with your inner world.

Use phrases like:

1. *"I embrace imperfection as a stepping stone toward growth and self-improvement."*
2. *"Mistakes are opportunities in disguise, leading me toward greater wisdom."*
3. *"I give myself permission to learn from my missteps and evolve."*
4. *"Every error I make is a chance to become better, wiser, and more resilient."*
5. *"I choose self-compassion over self-criticism, even in the face of mistakes."*
6. *"Mistakes do not define me; they are merely moments in my journey."*
7. *"I release the need for perfection and welcome the freedom to learn from my errors."*
8. *"Each mistake is a brushstroke on the canvas of my experience, creating a unique masterpiece."*
9. *"I value the lessons hidden within my mistakes, for they guide me toward my true potential."*
10. *"I forgive myself for any missteps and move forward with newfound wisdom."*

Positive Visualization Table

Goal	Visualization Details	Positive Affirmations	Emotions Felt

Day 10
Confronting Your People-Pleaser

Date _____

This archetype often involves a strong desire to gain approval and avoid conflict at the cost of one's own needs and boundaries.

Outcome:

You'll have a deeper understanding of your People-Pleaser tendencies and how they impact your life. This self-awareness is the first step toward transforming this shadow aspect into healthier patterns of interaction.

Exercises:

Self-Reflection: Throughout the day, pay attention to situations where your People-Pleaser tendencies emerge. Note the specific instances, thoughts, and actions you take to please others, even when it doesn't align with your true desires. For example, *"2:00 PM — Said 'yes' to extra work even though I already had a full plate."*

People-Pleaser Journaling: In the evening, dedicate a journal entry to your People-Pleaser. Write down the moments when you put others' needs before your own. Explore the underlying reasons and emotions that drive this behavior.

Setting Boundaries: Practice setting clear boundaries when appropriate. Say 'no' when you genuinely can't accommodate others' requests without neglecting your well-being.

Examples:

Self-Reflection: You might notice that your People-Pleaser tendencies surface when a friend asks for your help, and you say 'yes,' even though you're exhausted and need time for self-care. Your inner dialogue may involve thoughts like, *"I can't let them down."*

People-Pleaser Journaling: In your journal, you write, *"I agreed to help a friend even though I needed rest. My fear of disappointing them is what drove my decision. I recognize the need to balance their needs with my own."*

Remember:

Day 10 is dedicated to exploring the People-Pleaser within you. As you reflect, journal, and practice setting boundaries, you'll begin to uncover the roots of this shadow aspect and initiate the process of transformation toward a more balanced and authentic way of interacting with others.

People-Pleaser Journaling

Situation	What I Did	Emotions	Underlying Reasons	Self-Reflection	Lesson Learned

Day 11
Unveiling Your Inner Control Freak

Date _____

We'll shift our focus to another prevalent shadow aspect: the Control Freak. This inner aspect often seeks to maintain control in various situations, which can lead to anxiety and strained relationships. Today, we aim to identify and understand your inner Control Freak.

Outcome:

By the end of Day, you will have a clearer awareness of the presence of your Control Freak aspect and how it influences your thoughts and behaviors. This understanding is the initial step towards integrating this shadow aspect.

Exercises:

Self-Reflection: Throughout the day, pay attention to moments when your inner Control Freak emerges. Note the specific situations, thoughts, and controlling behaviors that surface. For example, *"3:00 PM — Control Freak emerged when a project wasn't going as planned."*

Control Freak Journaling: In the evening, dedicate a journal entry to your Control Freak aspect. Write down the controlling thoughts and actions you observed during the day. Challenge these behaviors with more flexible and relaxed responses.

Affirmation: In addition to the exercises, use affirmations to counteract your Control Freak's need for control. Affirmations can help you embrace flexibility and ease in various situations.

Examples:

Self-Reflection: You might notice your inner Control Freak appearing when plans don't go as expected. It compels you to micromanage and become anxious.

Control Freak Journaling: You write down, *"My Control Freak aspect emerged when the project went off track. I challenge this by reminding myself that not everything needs to be perfect. Adaptability is key to reducing stress."*

Remember:

As you observe and journal about its influence on your thoughts and behaviors, you'll take the initial step towards understanding and ultimately integrating this facet of your shadow.

Control Freak Journaling

Situation/Trigger	Controlling Thoughts and Actions	Flexible and Relaxed Responses

Affirmation

Here are 20 affirmations to counteract the Control Freak aspect's need for control:

I release the need to control everything in my life.

I trust that things will work out as they should.

Flexibility is my superpower, and I embrace it.

I allow space for spontaneity and creativity.

I let go of my desire to micromanage every detail.

I am at ease with uncertainty and change.

I find peace in surrendering control.

I focus on the big picture rather than getting caught up in details.

I adapt to new situations with grace and composure.

I release the grip of perfectionism.

I am open to others' input and ideas.

I choose to go with the flow of life.

I trust myself and my ability to handle challenges.

I am relaxed and composed in all situations.

I am free from the need to dominate conversations.

I welcome diversity of thought and perspective.

I value collaboration and teamwork.

I am patient with myself and others.

I find joy in giving up control and experiencing life fully.

I embrace the beauty of unpredictability.

Repeat these affirmations regularly to reprogram your mindset and cultivate a more flexible and relaxed approach to life, countering the Control Freak aspect's influence.

Day 12
Unveiling Your Victim Archetype

Date _____

Today's focus shifts to another shadow aspect, the Victim. The Victim archetype can often leave us feeling helpless and disempowered. Our aim is to identify and understand this aspect.

Outcome:

By the end of the day, you will have a clearer awareness of your Victim archetype's presence and how it influences your thoughts and behaviors. This awareness is the initial step in integrating this shadow aspect.

Exercises:

Self-Reflection: Throughout the day, pay attention to moments when your Victim archetype emerges. Note the specific situations, thoughts, and self-pitying language it uses. For example, *"3:00 PM — Victim archetype surfaced when I faced a minor setback."*

Victim Journaling: In the evening, dedicate a journal entry to your Victim archetype. Write down the self-pitying thoughts you observed during the day. Challenge these thoughts with self-empowering responses.

Affirmation: In addition to the exercises, use affirmations to counteract your Victim archetype's disempowering self-talk. Affirmations are positive statements that can help shift your mindset.

Examples:

Self-Reflection: You might notice that your Victim archetype appears when facing adversity. It tells you that life is always unfair and nothing ever goes your way.

Victim Journaling: You write down, *"My Victim archetype tells me that life is unfair. I challenge this thought by reminding myself that I have the power to overcome challenges and create positive outcomes."*

Remember:

By observing and journaling about its influence on your thoughts and feelings, you'll begin the process of understanding and ultimately integrating this aspect of your shadow.

Victim Journaling

Situation or Trigger	Self-Pitying Thoughts	Self-Empowering Responses

Affirmation

Here are 20 affirmations to counteract the disempowering self-talk associated with the Victim archetype:

I am resilient and can overcome life's challenges.

I have the power to change my circumstances.

I choose to focus on solutions, not problems.

I am in control of my thoughts and emotions.

I am strong, capable, and resourceful.

I release self-pity and embrace self-empowerment.

I can learn and grow from setbacks.

I choose to see opportunities in every situation.

I deserve happiness and success.

I am the author of my own story.

I am not defined by my past or mistakes.

I take responsibility for my choices and actions.

I have an abundance of inner strength.

I believe in my ability to create a brighter future.

I am resilient in the face of adversity.

I let go of self-victimization and embrace self-empowerment.

I am worthy of love, respect, and success.

I focus on the present and create a better tomorrow.

I am the master of my fate and the captain of my soul.

I choose self-empowerment over self-pity.

These affirmations can help shift your mindset from a victim mentality to one of empowerment and resilience. You can choose the ones that resonate most with you or create your own tailored to your specific needs.

Day 13
Healing through Forgiveness

Date

Forgiveness is a profound step toward healing emotional wounds and achieving inner peace. During these three days, you will focus on forgiving others, forgiving yourself, and understanding the healing potential of this powerful practice.

Outcome:

By the end of this day, you will have a deeper understanding of forgiveness and its role in shadow work. You'll begin the process of forgiving others, setting the stage for self-forgiveness and inner healing over the next two days.

Exercises:

Day One: Forgiving Others

Letter of Forgiveness to Others: Write a heartfelt letter of forgiveness to someone who has hurt you in the past. Be open and honest about your feelings and experiences, and express your willingness to let go of any resentment.

Reflective Journaling — Letting Go: Spend time in reflective journaling, focusing on the act of letting go through forgiveness. Share your insights, your decision to forgive, and the emotional release you experience.

Guided Forgiveness Meditation: Find a quiet and comfortable space to engage in a guided forgiveness meditation. Visualize the act of forgiving others and releasing the burden of resentment. Allow feelings of compassion and understanding to flow.

Examples:

Reflective Journaling — Letting Go: *Today, I took the first step in forgiving someone who hurt me. It wasn't easy, but I can already feel a sense of relief. Forgiveness is not about condoning the actions but about releasing the hold they have on my well-being.*

Guided Forgiveness Meditation: *During the meditation, I pictured the person I needed to forgive. As I extended forgiveness, I felt a sense of freedom and lightness. It's a significant start to this three-day journey of healing through forgiveness.*

Remember:

Forgiveness is a process, and these three days are the beginning of a transformative journey towards healing and inner peace.

Letter of Forgiveness to Others

Dear [*Recipient's Name*],

I hope this letter finds you in good health and peace. I have taken the time to write to you because there is something I've been carrying within me, and I believe it's time to release it.

I want you to know that I have decided to forgive you for [*briefly describe the specific situation or actions that hurt you*]. This is not about excusing or justifying what happened; it's about letting go of the burden of resentment that has weighed me down.

Carrying this pain has affected me in ways I didn't fully realize. It's hindered my own peace and happiness. I believe that forgiveness is a gift I can give not only to you but, more importantly, to myself.

I understand that we all make mistakes and can sometimes hurt others unintentionally. I choose to extend compassion and understanding to you. I release any grudge or negative feelings I've held against you.

Forgiveness is a powerful act of self-healing, and in forgiving you, I am taking a step toward my own emotional freedom and well-being. I hope that you, too, find peace and healing on your own journey.

Thank you for reading this letter, and I wish you the best on your path.

Sincerely,

[*Your Name*]

Reflective Journaling on Letting Go through Forgiveness

Forgiveness Focus: [Specify the situation or, person that you're working on forgiving.] _____

_____

_____

Insights: [Share your insights about the need for forgiveness in this situation. What has led you to this point?] _____

_____

_____

Decision to Forgive: [Explain your decision to forgive. What motivated you to make this choice?] _____

_____

_____

The Act of Letting Go: [Describe how the process of forgiveness felt. Did you experience a sense of release or relief? _____

_____

_____

Emotional Experience: [Reflect on the emotions you encountered during this process. Did you feel anger, resentment, or sadness, and did they transform into something else?] _____

_____

_____

Self-Reflection: [Consider the impact of forgiveness on your well-being, relationships, and personal growth. How has this practice changed you?] _____

_____

_____

Closing Remarks: [Conclude your journal entry with any closing thoughts, gratitude, or intentions for future forgiveness work.] _____

_____

_____

Day 14
Healing through Forgiveness

Date _____

In the next three days, we will continue to explore the process of forgiveness. Today's focus is on self-forgiveness, a crucial step in releasing the emotional burdens that can hold us back. It's a chance to let go of guilt and self-blame, fostering self-compassion and personal growth.

Outcome:

By the end of these three days, you will have a deeper understanding of the power of forgiveness, both towards others and yourself. You'll experience emotional release and find greater peace within.

Exercises:

Self-Forgiveness Letter: Write a letter to yourself, focusing on forgiving yourself for past mistakes or actions that have caused guilt. Be compassionate and understanding in your words.

Guided Meditation for Self-Forgiveness: Engage in a guided meditation or visualization specifically designed for self-forgiveness. Use it as a tool to release self-blame and cultivate self-compassion.

Self-Forgiveness Journaling: Spend time journaling about your journey to self-forgiveness. Reflect on the letter you wrote to yourself and your experience during the guided meditation.

Examples:

Self-Forgiveness Letter: Begin your letter with *"Dear [Your Name]," and express forgiveness for specific actions or situations that have been causing you guilt. For example, "I forgive myself for the mistakes I made in my previous relationship."*

Guided Meditation for Self-Forgiveness: Use a meditation app or recording that guides you through the process of self-forgiveness. Visualize releasing guilt and embracing self-compassion.

Self-Forgiveness Journaling: In your journal, you might write about the emotions that surfaced during the self-forgiveness exercises, any insights gained, and your commitment to letting go of self-blame.

Remember:

Forgiveness is a process, and it may not happen all at once. Be patient with yourself and continue to practice self-forgiveness regularly for lasting change.

Self-Forgiveness Letter

[Your Name]

[Date]

Dear [Your Name],

I write this letter to you with an open heart and the intention of forgiveness. I know that there are moments in our past that have burdened you with guilt, regret, and self-blame. Today, I want to release you from the weight of those emotions and offer you forgiveness.

I forgive you for the mistakes you made in your past, for the times you stumbled and made choices that hurt yourself or others. I understand that you did the best you could with the knowledge and resources you had at that time. You were navigating through life, learning, and growing.

I forgive you for the moments of weakness and vulnerability when you let fear and doubt cloud your judgment. It's okay to have been human, with flaws and imperfections. I embrace those imperfections as part of what makes you unique and beautiful.

I forgive you for the times you held onto grudges and resentment, which only hurt you more than anyone else. It's time to let go of the pain and anger you've been carrying. In forgiveness, we find freedom.

I forgive you for any harsh self-criticism, negative self-talk, or the belief that you were not enough. You are enough, just as you are. Your worth is not determined by your past actions or mistakes.

Today, I release you from the chains of self-blame. I let go of the guilt that has held you captive. I extend my compassion and understanding, knowing that you are worthy of forgiveness and love.

I promise to continue this journey of self-forgiveness, to practice self-compassion, and to treat you with kindness and respect. We are in this together, and we are evolving.

With love and forgiveness,

[Your Name]

Self-Forgiveness Journal

Situation or Mistake	Emotions & Thoughts	Self-Forgiveness Process	Outcomes and Insights

Day 15
Navigating Shadow Revelations in Relationships

Date _____

Today, we shift our focus to navigating shadow revelations within the context of your relationships. Shadow work often uncovers hidden aspects that influence how you interact with others. Understanding these dynamics is crucial for healthier and more authentic relationships.

Outcome:

By the end of this day, you will have a better grasp of how your shadow aspects affect your interactions with others and develop strategies for more authentic and harmonious relationships.

Exercises:

Reflecting on Relationship Patterns: Examine your relationships, both past and present. Identify any recurring patterns or challenges you've encountered. Note the emotions and behaviors that emerge in these dynamics.

Identifying Shadow Projections: Recognize instances where you project your shadow aspects onto others. Pay attention to moments when you see qualities or behaviors in someone else that trigger a strong emotional reaction in you.

Journaling Your Insights: Dedicate time to journal about your insights regarding relationship patterns and shadow projections. Explore how your concealed qualities influence your interactions.

Inner Dialogue with Your Shadow: Engage in an inner dialogue exercise, conversing with your shadow aspects regarding your relationships. Ask them how they contribute to your relationship dynamics and what they need to feel acknowledged.

Examples:

Reflecting on Relationship Patterns Example: If you've noticed a pattern of feeling abandoned or unimportant in your past relationships, this exercise can reveal a concealed fear of abandonment that influences your interactions.

Identifying Shadow Projections Example: You may find that you become irritated when a coworker displays arrogance and confidence. This strong reaction could indicate that you're projecting your own concealed insecurities onto them.

Journaling Your Insights Example: Through journaling, you may uncover that your concealed control issues lead to a pattern of micromanaging your team at work. This realization can prompt a shift in your leadership style.

Inner Dialogue with Your Shadow Example: During the inner dialogue exercise, you ask your shadow aspects why you react defensively in certain arguments with your partner. Your shadow reveals that it's protecting your vulnerability by using defensiveness as a shield.

This day invites you to explore the impact of your shadow aspects on your relationships. Understanding these dynamics can lead to healthier, more authentic interactions with others.

Reflecting on Relationship Patterns

Relationship Patterns	Recurring Challenges	Emotions and Behaviors

Identifying Shadow Projections

Situation/Person	Qualities/Behaviors Projected	Emotional Reaction

Journaling Your Insights

Insights on Relationship Patterns	Insights on Shadow Projections

Inner Dialogue with Your Shadow

An inner dialogue with your shadow aspects should be a compassionate and reflective conversation. Here's a general structure to follow:

1. **Set the Scene:**
   Find a quiet and comfortable space where you won't be disturbed.

2. **Address Your Shadow Aspect:**
   Imagine this aspect as a separate part of you with its own voice.

3. **Start the Dialogue:**
   Ask open-ended questions. For example:
   "What role do you play in my relationships?"
   "What motivates your actions and behaviors in these interactions?"
   "What do you need or seek to achieve?"

4. **Listen Actively:**
   Allow your shadow aspect to respond. Avoid judgment or criticism.

5. **Seek Common Ground:**
   Find common ground between your conscious self and your shadow aspect. Understand the positive intentions behind its actions.

6. **Provide Reassurance and Acknowledgment:**
   Offer understanding and validation for your shadow's needs and concerns. Assure it that you're working toward a more balanced and integrated self.

7. **Set Intentions:**
   Express your intention to work together as a team, acknowledging that both your conscious self and your shadow aspects have valid contributions to make.

8. **Reflect and Take Action:**
   Reflect on the insights gained during the dialogue.
   Consider how you can apply this understanding to improve your relationships.

Day 16
Embracing Your Inner Light

Date _____

Today's focus is on recognizing and embracing your inner light, which represents your strengths, virtues, and positive qualities. It's about acknowledging that you are more than your shadows, and you possess the potential for growth, healing, and self-empowerment.

Outcome:

You'll have a deeper understanding of your inner light and how it can guide you toward personal growth and self-empowerment. You'll recognize the strengths and virtues that can help you overcome challenges and lead a more fulfilling life.

Exercises:

Inner Light Inventory: List your positive qualities, strengths, and virtues. Reflect on times when these qualities have shone through in your life.

Empowerment Affirmations: Create affirmations that emphasize your strengths and virtues. Use these affirmations as reminders of your inner light.

Examples:

Inner Light Inventory Example: Recognize qualities such as kindness, resilience, courage, and wisdom within yourself. Reflect on moments when you've demonstrated these strengths.

Empowerment Affirmations Example: Develop affirmations like *"I am resilient and capable of overcoming any challenge"* or *"My kindness and empathy make a positive impact on those around me."*

Inner Light Inventory

Positive Qualities, Strengths, and Virtues	Moments when these qualities have shone through

Empowerment Affirmations

Here are 20 Empowerment Affirmations:

I am a beacon of light, radiating positivity and warmth.

My strength and resilience guide me through life's challenges.

My creativity knows no bounds, and I express it freely.

I am patient, allowing life to unfold in its own time.

My courage leads me to face fears and seize opportunities.

I empathize deeply, connecting with others on a profound level.

Wisdom flows through me, enriching my decisions and actions.

Kindness is a part of who I am, and I share it with the world.

My integrity shines brightly in all that I do.

I persevere with determination, achieving my goals.

My self-worth is unwavering and radiates from within.

I trust in my inner guidance and follow my intuition.

Love and compassion guide my interactions with others.

I am a source of inspiration to those around me.

Abundance and success flow into my life effortlessly.

My confidence empowers me to pursue my dreams.

I attract positivity and good fortune into my life.

I am resilient and capable of overcoming any obstacle.

Every day, I step into my power and embrace my inner light.

I am a shining example of authenticity and self-expression.

These affirmations are designed to empower individuals by highlighting their strengths and virtues.

Day 17
Exploring Self-Expression

Date _____

Today, you will explore your capacity for self-expression and its role in your life. It's a day dedicated to understanding how you communicate, both verbally and non-verbally, and how it impacts your relationships, personal growth, and self-awareness.

Outcome:

By the end of this day, you should have a clearer understanding of your self-expression patterns, whether they are assertive or passive, and how they influence your interactions with others and your overall well-being.

Exercises:

Self-Expression Awareness: Reflect on your communication style. Are you generally assertive, passive, or somewhere in between? Note specific situations where your self-expression style has been helpful or challenging.

Journal Your Communication: Keep a journal throughout the day to document your communication. Record conversations, text messages, or any form of self-expression. Analyze whether your communication aligns with your true thoughts and feelings.

Role-Playing Exercise: Engage in a role-playing exercise with a friend or a journal. Act out a situation where you express yourself assertively. Then, try the same scenario with passive communication. Compare your experiences and the responses you receive.

Examples:

Self-Expression Awareness Example: You realize that you tend to be passive during team meetings at work. You avoid sharing your ideas even when you believe they could benefit the team's project.

Journal Your Communication Example: During a conversation with a friend, you notice that you downplayed your true feelings about a situation to avoid conflict. You wrote this interaction in your journal for later reflection.

Role-Playing Exercise Example: You role-play a scenario with a friend, expressing assertively what you'd like to eat for dinner. Then, you replay the scenario with passive communication, deferring to your friend's choice. You compare the responses and your own feelings during both interactions.

Remember:

Exploring self-expression is a crucial part of shadow work, as it can help you understand how your communication patterns relate to your inner self and the personas you present to the world. Continue this exploration in the coming days to gain further insights into your self-expression style.

Journal Your Communication

Communication Type: [Conversation, text message, email, etc.]

Communication Partner: [Name of the person you communicated with.]

Content of Communication: [Briefly describe the main topic of the conversation or message.]

Your Self-Expression: [Describe how you expressed yourself in this interaction (assertive, passive, or other).]

Reflection: [Analyze whether your communication in this instance aligned with your true thoughts and feelings. Were there any discrepancies? How did you feel about this communication?]

Feel free to use this template to keep a record of your daily communications and reflections, helping you gain insights into your self-expression patterns and their alignment with your authentic self.

Role-Playing Exercise

Here's an example of a role-playing exercise:

Scenario: Requesting a Day Off

You: (In the role of the employee)

Assertive Communication:

You approach your supervisor with confidence and say, *"I'd like to request a day off next week because I have a family event to attend. I've planned it in advance, and I believe my work can be managed during my absence. Is it possible for me to take that day off?"*

Passive Communication:

You hesitantly approach your supervisor and say, *"Um, I was thinking... next week, there's this family thing, and I thought, maybe, it's not that important, but, um, could I possibly, perhaps, have that day off if it's not too much trouble?"*

Friend or Journal (In the role of the supervisor)

After the Assertive Communication:

Responds positively, appreciates your upfront approach, and agrees to your day off.

After the Passive Communication:

Expresses confusion due to the unclear request and asks for clarification. Might delay or deny the request due to the lack of clarity.

After this role-play exercise, reflect on your experiences and the responses received in each scenario. Discuss the differences in how you felt and the outcomes in terms of assertive versus passive communication. This exercise helps you understand the impact of your communication style on your interactions.

Day 18
Healing through Self-Expression

Date _____

This day focuses on the power of self-expression and how it can help you heal and grow. It's about discovering healthy ways to communicate your thoughts, emotions, and needs.

Outcome:

By the end of this day, you'll gain a deeper understanding of how self-expression can contribute to your healing and personal growth. You'll explore various forms of self-expression and their benefits.

Exercises:

Emotional Journaling: Dedicate some time to journaling about your emotions. Write freely without judgment or criticism. Explore what you're feeling and why. This practice can help you release pent-up emotions.

Creative Expression: Engage in a creative activity, whether it's art, writing, music, or any other form of artistic expression. Use this as a means to convey your emotions and thoughts.

Mindful Conversation: Have a mindful conversation with a friend, partner, or family member. Focus on active listening and assertive communication. Share your feelings and needs honestly and openly.

Examples:

Emotional Journaling: Take a few minutes to write about how you're feeling today. For instance, *"I'm feeling anxious because of a work deadline, and I'm worried about not meeting it."*

Creative Expression: Paint a picture that represents your current emotional state. Use colors, shapes, and patterns that reflect your feelings.

Mindful Conversation: Speak with a friend about something that has been bothering you. Use active listening skills, and openly express how their actions or words have affected you.

Emotional Journaling

Emotions You Felt	Trigger or Cause	Notes

Creative Expression

Mindful Conversaton. Notes

Day 19
Exploring Resistance

Date _____

Resistance often stands in the way of personal growth and transformation. It's the internal force that prevents you from making changes or facing uncomfortable truths. Today, you will explore the resistance you've encountered on your shadow work path.

Outcome:

By the end of the day, you'll have a better understanding of the areas in your life where resistance shows up. You'll identify patterns of avoidance and reluctance. Recognizing your resistance is the first step to overcoming it and moving forward in your shadow work.

Exercises:

Resistance Identification: Reflect on your shadow work journey so far. When have you felt resistant to certain tasks, self-reflection, or inner exploration? Make a list of these instances, noting the specific situations, emotions, and thoughts that accompanied them.

Resistance Journaling: Dedicate a journaling session to explore your resistance. Write about the situations or aspects of your shadow work that trigger resistance. Examine the thoughts and emotions that arise when you encounter resistance.

Resistance Role-Play: Engage in a role-play exercise with a friend or in your journal. Act out a scenario where resistance emerges. Then, switch roles to play the part of the person who overcomes that resistance. This exercise can help you understand the dynamics at play when resistance arises.

Examples:

Resistance Identification Example: Recall a time during your shadow work when you felt strong resistance to confronting a specific shadow aspect. Note the circumstances, emotions, and thoughts that made you resist this work.

Resistance Journaling Example: Write about a recent situation in your shadow work where resistance was palpable. Describe the resistance you felt and the inner dialogue that occurred as a result.

Resistance Role-Play Example: In a journal entry or with a friend, reenact a situation where you resisted shadow work or self-reflection. Then, replay the scenario where you overcome that resistance and engage in the work willingly.

Remember:

Exploring resistance is a crucial step in your shadow work journey. It will help you uncover the barriers that have held you back and allow you to move past them.

Resistance Journaling

Trigger or Situation	Emotions Experienced	Thoughts and Inner Dialogue	Insights or Reflections

Resistance Role-Play

Here's an example of a Resistance Role-Play exercise:

Scenario:

Imagine you've set a goal to start a daily meditation practice as part of your shadow work journey. You've encountered resistance, and it's preventing you from meditating consistently.

Role-Play:

Role of Resistance: You play the part of yourself as Resistance. Express your thoughts and emotions that are holding you back. For example: *"I don't have time for meditation. It's too hard to sit still. I'm too restless for this."*

Role of Overcoming Resistance: Now, switch roles and play the part of the person who successfully overcomes resistance. Address the Resistance character's concerns with assertive and self-compassionate responses. For example: *"I understand you're busy, but meditation can actually help you focus better. It's okay to feel restless; that's normal. Just start with a few minutes and gradually build your practice."*

Reflect: After completing the role-play, reflect on the experience. Write down any insights you gained from taking on both roles. How did it feel to overcome resistance? What did you learn about the nature of your resistance?

This exercise helps you identify and address the thoughts and emotions that contribute to resistance, allowing you to develop strategies to overcome it and make progress in your shadow work.

Day 20
Honoring Your Progress

Date _____

Honoring your achievements, no matter how small they may seem, is an important part of self-compassion and self-acknowledgment.

Outcome:

By the end of this day, you should have a deeper appreciation for the progress you've made in your shadow work. Recognizing your growth and self-awareness can boost your motivation and confidence as you continue your journey.

Exercises:

Reflection on Progress: Take some time to reflect on your shadow work journey so far. Write down the areas where you've made noticeable progress. These could be improvements in self-awareness, changes in your thought patterns, or the ability to recognize and address your shadow aspects.

Celebratory Ritual: Create a simple and meaningful ritual to celebrate your progress. This could involve lighting a candle, taking a nature walk, or any other activity that feels symbolic of your journey. During this ritual, express gratitude to yourself for the commitment and effort you've invested in your personal growth.

Examples:

Reflection on Progress Example: *"During this shadow work journey, I've become more aware of my inner critic's influence, and I've started to counteract its negative self-talk with self-compassion. I've also identified some of my shadow aspects and worked on integrating them."*

Celebratory Ritual Example: You might choose to light a candle, sit quietly, and express your gratitude to yourself. You could say, *"I am proud of the progress I've made. I acknowledge my commitment to self-improvement, and I am grateful for the insights and growth I've experienced."*

Honoring your progress is a vital step in shadow work, as it reinforces your motivation and self-compassion, helping you stay dedicated to your journey of self-discovery and healing.

Reflection on Progress

Progress Area	Notable Improvements

Day 21
Gratitude and Self-Reflection

Date _____

Today, we'll focus on the power of gratitude in your shadow work journey. Gratitude can be a transformative force, helping you appreciate your progress and maintain a positive outlook. We'll combine gratitude with self-reflection to deepen your understanding of your inner world.

Outcome:

By the end of this day, you'll have cultivated a sense of gratitude for your journey, your growth, and the lessons you've learned. Self-reflection will provide you with insights into your evolving relationship with your shadow aspects.

Exercises:

Gratitude Journaling: Take time to write down at least five things you're grateful for today. They can be related to your shadow work or any other aspect of your life. Reflect on how these sources of gratitude have impacted your overall well-being.

Self-Reflection: In your journal, reflect on the changes you've noticed in your relationship with your shadow aspects throughout this journey.
Examine how your understanding, acceptance, and integration of these aspects have evolved.

Guided Gratitude Meditation: Find a quiet space and engage in a guided gratitude meditation. Focus on the positive aspects of your life and your inner growth.

Examples:

Gratitude Journaling: *"Today, I'm grateful for the support of my friends and family, the lessons I've learned through my shadow work, the ability to acknowledge my inner critic without judgment, the strength I've found within me, and the opportunity to grow and evolve."*

Self-Reflection: *"Throughout this shadow work process, I've observed a significant shift in how I perceive my inner critic. I used to resent and suppress it, but now I've learned to see it as a part of me, a reminder of my vulnerability, and a source of potential growth. Accepting and integrating it has reduced my self-criticism."*

Guided Gratitude Meditation: Follow a guided gratitude meditation audio or video, focusing on your journey and the positive aspects that have emerged from your shadow work.

On this day, combine the practices of gratitude and self-reflection to reinforce the progress you've made and to appreciate the transformative journey you're on.

Gratitude Journaling

Gratitude List	Impact on Well-Being

Self-Reflection

Reflection on Shadow Work Progress	Changes Noticed

Day 22
The Power of Self-Compassion

Date _____

Self-compassion is the act of treating oneself with the same kindness and understanding that you would offer to a friend. This practice helps you to be more gentle and forgiving toward yourself, especially in moments when your shadow aspects or past mistakes come to the forefront.

Outcome:

By the end of this day, you will have a deeper understanding of self-compassion and its role in your shadow work journey. You will have practical tools to be more compassionate towards yourself as you continue to explore and integrate your shadow aspects.

Exercises:

Self-Compassion Meditation: Practice a self-compassion meditation. Sit quietly, focus on your breath, and gently repeat self-compassionate phrases, such as *"May I be kind to myself"* or *"I am deserving of love and compassion."*

Letter of Self-Compassion: Write a heartfelt letter to yourself, demonstrating self-compassion. Acknowledge your imperfections and struggles, and offer yourself words of understanding and encouragement.

Positive Self-Talk: Throughout the day, observe your self-talk. Whenever you notice self-criticism, reframe it with self-compassion. For example, if you find yourself saying, *"I'm such a failure,"* rephrase it as, *"I made a mistake, and that's okay. I can learn from it."*

Examples:

Self-Compassion Meditation Example: Find a quiet space, sit comfortably, and close your eyes. Take a few deep breaths to center yourself. As you breathe in and out, repeat some phrases in your mind:

Positive Self-Talk Example: Throughout the day, you notice a harsh self-criticism arising after a small mistake at work. You reframe your self-talk and say to yourself, *"I made an error, but that doesn't define my worth. I can learn from this experience and do better next time."*

These exercises and examples will guide you to embrace self-compassion as a powerful tool in your shadow work journey.

Self-Compassion Meditation

Here are 20 phrases for your self-compassion meditation:

May I be kind to myself.

I am deserving of love and compassion.

I accept myself as I am.

May I find peace in my heart.

I am worthy of self-care.

May I forgive myself for my mistakes.

I am gentle with myself in times of pain.

May I be patient with my imperfections.

I am understanding of my struggles.

May I be at ease with my fears.

I am open to self-acceptance.

May I embrace my inner strengths.

I am nurturing my inner child.

May I offer myself the gift of self-compassion.

I am my own source of comfort.

May I release self-judgment.

I am free from self-criticism.

May I grant myself the kindness I deserve.

I am a vessel of self-love.

May I let go of self-doubt.

Use these phrases in your self-compassion meditation to cultivate a kinder and more loving relationship with yourself.

Letter of Self-Compassion

[Your Name],

[Date]

Dear [Your Name],

I wanted to take a moment to acknowledge the incredible journey you've been on. Life has presented its share of challenges, and you've faced them with remarkable strength and resilience. I understand that you've made mistakes, felt vulnerable, and encountered moments of self-doubt. But I want you to know that it's okay.

You are deserving of love and kindness, especially from yourself. Your imperfections do not define you; they make you beautifully human. It's through your struggles that you've grown, learned, and become the person you are today.

Please remember to be gentle with yourself, just as you would be with a dear friend. Your worth is not measured by external standards or the opinions of others. You are enough just as you are, and you are worthy of self-compassion.

In times of pain, offer yourself the same comfort you'd give to a loved one. Forgive yourself for past missteps and let go of self-judgment. May you find peace in your heart and nurture your inner child with kindness.

You are a source of love and compassion, and it's time to turn some of that love inward. Embrace your inner strengths, and know that you are indeed deserving of self-care.

With understanding, acceptance, and love,

[Your Name]

Feel free to personalize this template and add your own experiences and emotions. This letter is for you, so make it as heartfelt as you'd like.

Day 23
Embracing Inner Wisdom

Date _____

This inner knowing is often obscured by the noise of daily life and the shadows that linger within us. By uncovering and trusting your inner wisdom, you can make more conscious choices and lead a life in alignment with your true self.

Outcome:

By the end of this day, you'll have a clearer understanding of your inner wisdom and how to access it. You'll recognize the guidance it offers and how to apply it to various aspects of your life.

Exercises:

Inner Wisdom Reflection:

- Find a quiet, comfortable space.
- Close your eyes, take several deep breaths, and focus on relaxing.
- When you feel centered, ask yourself a question or seek guidance on a current life challenge.
- Listen to the quiet voice of your inner wisdom.
- Reflect on the insights that arise during this meditation.

Journaling Your Inner Wisdom:

- Take out your journal.
- Write about a time when your inner wisdom guided you in making a significant decision.
- Reflect on the positive outcomes of trusting your inner wisdom.

Examples:

Inner Wisdom Reflection Example: Sit quietly, and ask your inner wisdom for guidance regarding a personal challenge. Let your thoughts and insights flow without judgment. You might receive answers or clarity you hadn't considered before.

Journaling Your Inner Wisdom Example: Write about a time when you had a significant decision to make, and your inner wisdom led you to the right choice. Describe the situation, the guidance you received, and the outcomes. Reflect on the difference trusting your inner wisdom made in your life.

Remember:

That this day is about tuning into your inner wisdom, which often speaks in subtle whispers. Be patient and open to receiving the insights that come your way. Trusting this guidance can be transformative in your shadow work journey.

Journaling Your Inner Wisdom

Significant Decision:	
How Did Your Inner Wisdom Guide You?	
Reflection on the Positive Outcomes:	

Significant Decision:	
How Did Your Inner Wisdom Guide You?	
Reflection on the Positive Outcomes:	

Significant Decision:	
How Did Your Inner Wisdom Guide You?	
Reflection on the Positive Outcomes:	

Significant Decision:	
How Did Your Inner Wisdom Guide You?	
Reflection on the Positive Outcomes:	

Significant Decision:	
How Did Your Inner Wisdom Guide You?	
Reflection on the Positive Outcomes:	

Significant Decision:	
How Did Your Inner Wisdom Guide You?	
Reflection on the Positive Outcomes:	

Day 24
Cultivating Compassion for Others

Date _____

Today, we turn our focus outward and work on cultivating compassion for others. Shadow work not only helps us understand ourselves better but also enhances our capacity to empathize with and be compassionate toward others. By developing a compassionate mindset, we can build healthier and more fulfilling relationships.

Outcome:

By the end of this day, you will have practiced and improved your ability to show compassion to others, even in challenging situations. This fosters stronger connections, more meaningful relationships, and a deeper sense of empathy.

Exercises:

Random Acts of Kindness: Throughout the day, perform random acts of kindness towards others. This could be as simple as holding the door for someone, offering a compliment, or helping a colleague. Reflect on how these acts make both you and the recipients feel.

Active Listening: Engage in a conversation with a friend, family member, or colleague. Practice active listening, where you give them your full attention, without judgment or interruption. Show empathy by acknowledging their emotions and concerns.

Compassion Meditation: Spend time meditating on compassion. Imagine sending waves of love and understanding to people you care about and even to those with whom you've had conflicts. Wish them happiness and freedom from suffering.

Examples:

Random Acts of Kindness: Pay for a stranger's coffee in line behind you. Compliment a coworker's hard work. Let someone with fewer items go ahead of you in the grocery store line.

Active Listening: Sit down with a friend who needs to talk about a personal challenge. As they share, listen attentively, offering supportive words. Avoid giving advice unless they explicitly ask for it.

Compassion Meditation: Find a quiet space to meditate. Picture the faces of loved ones and, one by one, send them thoughts of love, compassion, and happiness. Extend this meditation to include someone you may have conflicts with and genuinely wish them peace.

Remember:

Today's focus is on compassion for others, an integral part of shadow work, so embrace the opportunity to connect on a deeper level with those around you.

Summary

Exercises Completed:

Experiences and Feelings:

Overall Reflection:

How Do You Feel Now?:

Day 25
Embracing Change and Transformation

Date _____

Change can be daunting, but it's essential for growth. By exploring how you adapt to change and your willingness to embrace it, you'll uncover more about your shadow aspects and how they affect your relationship with transformation.

Outcome:

By the end of this day, you'll have a better understanding of your relationship with change and transformation. You'll recognize whether you tend to resist or welcome change and how this relates to your hidden aspects.

Now, let's move on to the exercises and examples:

Exercises:

Change Journaling: Spend some time in your journal reflecting on your experiences with change. Write about significant changes in your life and how you initially reacted to them. Explore the emotions, thoughts, and behaviors that arose during these transitions.

Your Shadow and Change: Reflect on how your shadow aspects influence your response to change. Do they create resistance, fear, or reluctance? Or do they facilitate adaptability and growth? Make notes on the role your shadow plays in your relationship with change.

Examples:

Change Journaling Example: Recall a time when you experienced a major life change, such as starting a new job or ending a long-term relationship. Write about your initial reaction and how your emotions evolved as you adjusted to the change. Consider whether your shadow aspects were supportive or resistant during this transition.

Your Shadow and Change Example: If you noticed a pattern of resisting change during your reflection, consider which specific shadow aspects contribute to this resistance. For instance, if fear or self-doubt surfaces during times of change, these aspects may be influencing your response. Recognizing this connection is a significant step toward embracing transformation.

Use these exercises and examples to explore your relationship with change and how your shadow aspects influence your adaptability and growth.

Change Journaling

Change Experience	Initial Reaction	Emotions	Thoughts	Behaviors

Shadow and Change Notes

Change Experience	Shadow's Role

Day 26
Embracing Wholeness

Date _____

In these final days of your shadow work journey, it's time to reflect on the progress you've made and focus on the concept of wholeness. Embracing your shadow aspects and integrating them is key to achieving a sense of inner wholeness. This day is dedicated to recognizing that you are a complex, multifaceted individual, and every part of you contributes to your unique self.

Outcome:

By the end of this day, you will have a greater understanding of your own complexity and a deep sense of wholeness. Embracing your shadow aspects as integral parts of yourself is a powerful step toward inner peace and self-acceptance.

Exercises:

Embracing Wholeness Journaling: Take some time in your journal to reflect on the various aspects of yourself. Write about the parts of you that you've uncovered during this shadow work journey, both the light and shadow elements. Describe how each aspect contributes to your unique self.

Archetypal Reflection: Review the archetypes you identified and worked with during your shadow work journey. Reflect on how each archetype has influenced your life and shaped your personality. Consider how they have contributed to your sense of wholeness.

Examples:

Embracing Wholeness Journaling Example: *"In this journaling session, I've thought about my shadow aspects and how they complement my conscious self. I recognize that my self-doubt, which I used to see as a flaw, actually serves as a reminder to strive for improvement. My anxiety, although challenging, has made me more empathetic toward others going through similar experiences. I embrace all these facets as integral to my unique personality."*

Archetypal Reflection Example: *"As I reflect on the archetypes I've explored in my shadow work, I see how the Hero archetype has pushed me to achieve my goals. The Mother archetype has nurtured my relationships, and the Sage archetype has encouraged my intellectual growth. These archetypes have worked in harmony, contributing to my sense of wholeness."*

Embracing Wholeness Journaling

Aspect of Self	Description	Contribution to My Unique Self

In the "Aspect of Self" column, list the different aspects of yourself you've uncovered during your shadow work. In the "Description" column, briefly describe each aspect, whether it's a shadow or light aspect. In the "Contribution to My Unique Self" column, reflect on how each aspect contributes to your sense of wholeness. This exercise will help you see the value in all aspects of yourself.

Archetypal Reflection

Archetype	Influence on My Life	Contribution to Wholeness

Day 27
Renewal and Integration

Date _____

On this day, you'll focus on the renewal and integration of your self-awareness and the wisdom you've gained throughout this shadow work journey. It's time to bring everything together and prepare to move forward as a more integrated and self-aware individual.

Outcome:

By the end of this day, you should have a sense of renewal and a deeper understanding of your inner self. You'll be better equipped to continue your journey with the knowledge and insights you've acquired.

Exercises:

Integration Reflection: Take some time in your journal to reflect on the insights you've gained throughout your shadow work journey. How have you integrated your shadow aspects into your conscious self? What have you learned about yourself? Note down any challenges you've overcome.

Renewal Ritual: Create a simple ritual that symbolizes your commitment to self-awareness and integration. This could involve lighting a candle, meditating, or simply taking a few moments of quiet reflection. This ritual serves as a reminder of your ongoing journey of self-discovery.

Setting Intentions: Write down your intentions for the future. What are your goals for continuing your shadow work, and how do you plan to maintain your self-awareness and integration? Setting clear intentions can help guide your path.

Examples:

Integration Reflection Example: *"I've learned to accept and integrate my shadow aspects, particularly my fear of failure. This awareness has allowed me to take more calculated risks in my life and embrace opportunities that I once shied away from."*

Renewal Ritual Example: *"I lit a candle in a quiet room and took a few moments to meditate. It felt like a symbolic renewal, a commitment to maintaining self-awareness and embracing all aspects of myself."*

Setting Intentions Example: *"My intention for the future is to continue my shadow work journey. I want to delve deeper into my hidden qualities and further integrate them into my conscious self. This will lead to greater self-acceptance and growth."*

Take your time with these exercises and reflect on your personal journey of self-discovery. This day marks the renewal of your commitment to self-awareness and integration.

Integration Reflection

Insights on Integration	What I've Learned About Myself	Challenges Overcome

Day 28
Reflection and Celebration

Date _____

It's time to reflect on your progress, the insights you've gained, and the transformation you've experienced. This day is dedicated to celebrating your commitment to personal growth and self-discovery.

Outcome:

By the end of this day, you will have a deep sense of reflection, pride in your accomplishments, and a stronger connection with your integrated self. You'll be prepared to take the final step of your shadow work journey.

Exercises:

Journal of Reflection: Spend time in your journal reflecting on the entire 28-day journey. Write about the most significant insights, changes, and challenges you've faced. Consider how you've grown during this process.

Letter of Self-Appreciation: Write a letter to yourself expressing appreciation for your dedication to shadow work and personal growth. Acknowledge your efforts and the courage it took to confront your shadow.

Take time to truly embrace your achievements today. You've come a long way in your shadow work journey. Tomorrow, you'll embark on the final day of this transformative process.

Journal of Reflection

Date	Reflection
Day 1	Reflect on the emotions and thoughts you experienced when you first began this journey. What were your expectations? How have they changed?
Day 5	Write about a significant insight you gained during the initial days. How did it affect your perspective on shadow work and self-discovery?
Day 10	Describe a specific challenge you faced during the middle of the journey. How did you overcome it, and what did you learn from that experience?
Day 15	Highlight any changes in your self-awareness. Has your relationship with your shadow aspects evolved?
Day 20	Consider the tools and techniques you've used in your journey. Which ones were most effective for you, and why?
Day 28	Reflect on the cumulative growth you've experienced. How do you perceive yourself now compared to day one of your shadow work journey?

In this journal, you can write down your thoughts, insights, and self-reflections for each of these days. It will help you track your progress and celebrate the transformative process you've undergone.

Letter of Self-Appreciation

Dear [Your Name],

I wanted to take a moment to express my deepest appreciation for the journey you've undertaken – the journey of self-discovery, growth, and confronting the shadows that reside within. You have demonstrated incredible dedication, courage, and resilience in this transformative process.

As you reflect on the path you've walked during these 30 days of shadow work, remember the moments when you faced your fears, confronted your inner critic, and embraced your inner child with compassion. Those weren't easy steps to take, but you did so with unwavering determination.

Your commitment to self-improvement and personal growth is truly commendable. Through the ups and downs, the moments of clarity, and the challenges that tested your resolve, you persisted. You showed up for yourself, day after day, and for that, I applaud you.

This journey is far from over, but it's essential to acknowledge how far you've come. You've gained insights that have deepened your self-awareness and illuminated your path towards wholeness. Your actions have helped you integrate your shadow aspects into your conscious self, creating a richer, more authentic you.

I want to emphasize that self-appreciation is not about perfection, but about recognizing and celebrating the journey itself. Each step you've taken has contributed to your growth and transformation. Continue to nurture self-compassion, and allow it to guide you through the ongoing exploration of your inner world.

I'm truly proud of your commitment to this process. Remember, the dedication you've shown on this path of self-discovery is a reflection of your strength and resilience. You have the capacity to embrace your shadows and let your inner light shine even brighter.

With deep appreciation,

[Your Name]

Feel free to use this template as a starting point for your Letter of Self-Appreciation. You can personalize it to match your own thoughts and feelings during your shadow work journey.

Exclusive BONUS

Congratulations on completing your journey through
"Shadow Work Journal." To aid you further on your path
to self-discovery and emotional healing, we're pleased
to offer an exclusive bonus.

Unveiling Guided Art Sessions

Access a series of expert-guided art sessions to deepen your
expressive healing practice. These sessions cover various
aspects of the transformative exercises discussed in the book.

To unlock this exclusive resource,
scan the QR code
below using your smartphone or tablet.

Expressive Healing:
**Art as Your Path
to Wholeness**

Made in the USA
Las Vegas, NV
06 January 2024

83988489R00083